A RIFT IN TIME

RAJA SHEHADEH is the author of the highly praised memoir *Strangers in the House*, and the enormously acclaimed *When the Bulbul Stopped Singing*, which was made into a stage play. He is a Palestinian lawyer and writer who lives in Ramallah. He is the founder of the pioneering, non-partisan human rights organisation Al-Haq, an affiliate of the International Commission of Jurists, and the author of several books about international law, human rights and the Middle East. His most recent book, *Palestinian Walks* won the Orwell Prize in 2008.

ALSO BY RAJA SHEHADEH

When the Bulbul Stopped Singing
Strangers in the House
Palestinian Walks

A RIFT IN TIME

Travels with My Ottoman Uncle

RAJA SHEHADEH

P

PROFILE BOOKS

First published in Great Britain in 2010 by
PROFILE BOOKS LTD
3A Exmouth House
Pine Street
London EC1R OJH
www.profilebooks.com

1 3 5 7 9 10 8 6 4 2

Typeset in Aldus by MacGuru Ltd
info@macguru.org.uk
Printed and bound in Great Britain by
Clays, Bungay, Suffolk

A CIP catalogue record for this book is available from the
British Library.

ISBN 978 1 84668 330 5
eISBN 978 1 84765 273 7

The paper this book is printed on is certified by the © 1996 Forest
Stewardship Council A.C. (FSC). It is ancient-forest friendly. The
printer holds FSC chain of custody SGS-COC-2061

FSC

Mixed Sources

Product group from well-managed
forests and other controlled sources

Cert no. SGS-COC-2061
www.fsc.org
© 1996 Forest Stewardship Council

To Widad, my mother, a story teller, who fell silent before she could find out the end of the story

'Human beings are capable of the unique trick, creating realities by first imagining them, by experiencing them in their minds. The active imagining somehow makes it real. And what is possible in the art becomes thinkable in life.'

Brian Eno

Contents

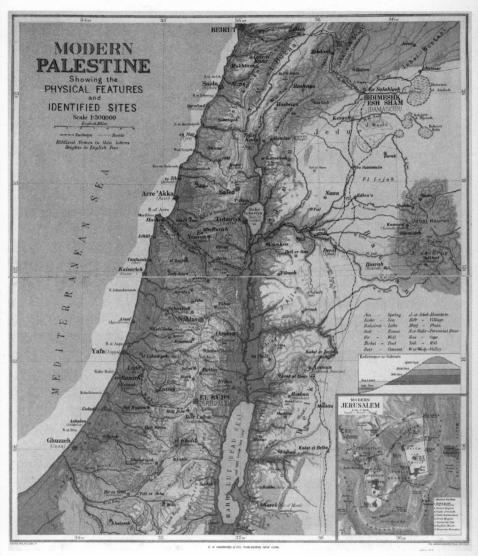

An undated, pre-1916 physical map of northern Palestine and neighbouring regions showing some of the towns, villages and areas mentioned in the text. (Courtesy of the Library of Congress.)

A RIFT IN TIME

Frontispiece: A Bedouin man and his horse at the Makhada in the Jordan River where Najib forded the river in the course of his great escape.

Escaping Arrest

'They're coming to arrest you,' Hanan, my sister-in-law, called to warn me in her strong, matter-of-fact voice. 'Samer is on his way.'

My mother had just called Hanan in a panic to dispatch my brother to my aid, convinced that the Palestinian security police would be at my door any minute. She was frantic. An anonymous official from the office of the Attorney General had rung her to ask about me because they did not have my phone number. Prudently, she refused to reveal it. 'Don't worry. We'll find him,' he had menacingly said before hanging up.

I wasted no time. I quickly put on thick underwear, tucked my toothbrush in a pocket and pulled on an extra sweater, prison survival tips learned from experienced security detainees I had represented in the past in Israeli military courts. Jericho, the site of the new Palestinian security prison and the old Israeli military government headquarters, can get very cold at night. On that evening of 18 September 1996 I sat huddled in the courtyard of our new house and waited for the knock on the door, trying to pretend I was neither worried nor angry.

Those first years of the transitional rule of the Palestinian Authority were strange times. It was the rude awakening at the end of a fascinating and hopeful period for me, during which I had devoted all my energies to bringing about change and a conclusion to the Israeli occupation. I had spent years challenging illegal Israeli land acquisitions in the occupied West Bank. Ironically, the unfounded claim that was now being made against my client was that he was selling land to the enemy by going into partnership with an Israeli corporation for the establishment of a gambling casino in Jericho, and I was accused of helping him with this venture. It was a false claim fabricated by some powerful members of the governing Authority who were hoping to intimidate my client into withdrawing from the project so that they could replace him in this lucrative enterprise.

Prompted perhaps by disappointment over the false peace heralded by the signing of the Oslo Accords, and despite all the fanfare on the White House lawn, my thoughts had been turning to the past, to the time when it all began. I had been reading about my great-great-uncle Najib Nassar, who like me was a writer, and like me a man whose hopes had been crushed when the Ottoman authority of his day sent troops to arrest him. But unlike me he did not wait for the knock on the door.

It was from my maternal grandmother, Julia, that I first heard of Najib. But he was always spoken of with ambivalence. He was the odd man out in the Nassar family, the one who was preoccupied with resistance politics during the British Mandate period while his brothers were making a good living, one as a hotelier, another as a medical doctor, a third as a pharmacist, all well-to-do, established members of the professional middle class, while he mingled with the *fellaheen*, the peasants, and lived for a while among them. Even worse, he associated with the Bedouins, spoke and dressed like them and generally adopted their ways. My grandmother told me about a visit he once made to the family home in the Mediterranean city of Haifa.

'We did not recognise him. We almost threw him out. Then he said, "I'm Najib." We could hardly believe it. He looked emaciated, all skin and bones. His beard was long and straggly, he wore a keffiyeh on his head and he smelt terribly, as he had been living out in the open. I will never forget that sight.'

Hearing this, I was intrigued. No one had mentioned the order for his arrest by the Ottoman government. I was left to wonder why he went to live out in the wild. What was he running away from? And why was he so poor? How did he lose his money? Did he gamble it away?

To locate the places where Najib found refuge during his long escape from the Ottoman police, I first used a map made by the Israeli Survey Department. But I soon discovered that, in the course of creating a new country over the ruins of the old, Israel had renamed almost every hill, spring and wadi in Palestine, striking from the map names and often habitations that had been there for centuries. It was the most frustrating endeavour. If only I could visit this area with someone able to read the landscape and point out where the old towns and villages had stood. I knew just the person, but the Palestinian geographer Kamal Abdulfattah was not allowed to cross into Israel from the West Bank. How Israel manages to complicate and frustrate every project!

After the failed attempt at mapping out Najib's escape route using a modern Israeli map, I managed to retrieve a 1933 map from the National Library of Scotland in Edinburgh. What a relief it was to look at this and envision the country Najib would have recognised, with the villages, hills and wadis in which he had taken refuge reassuringly marked and bearing the names that he had used.

In planning the route of his escape, Najib had not been hampered by the political borders that many Palestinians are not allowed to cross today. Under the Ottomans on the eve of the First World War there was no administrative unit called Palestine. Haifa, Acre, Safad and Tiberias were part of the Beirut *sanjaq* (an administrative subdivision of a *vilayet* or province). South of that, including Jaffa, Gaza and Jerusalem, was the independent *sanjaq* of Jerusalem. The south-eastern parts of Palestine were included in the *sanjaq* of Maan and all of these were part of the *vilayet* of Greater Syria. The River Jordan did not delineate a political border. Without delays Najib was able to ford it by horse and in no time found himself on the eastern bank in what today is the Hashemite Kingdom of Jordan. When he finally gave himself up he was transported by train to Damascus, a trip that took no longer than two hours. So distorted has the geography become that for us West Bank Palestinians to travel north to Damascus we would first have to travel east, then north, crossing four different countries; and even that is possible only if we are fortunate enough to secure the necessary visas and exit permits from often uncooperative authorities, both Israeli and Arab.

The quest for Najib – the details of his life and the route of his great escape – that consumed me for the next thirteen years was not an easy one. Most of Palestine's history, together with that of its people, is buried deep in the ground. To reconstruct the journey of my great-great-uncle I could not visit any of the houses where he and his family had lived in Haifa, his point of departure. This mixed community of Arabs and Jews has become an Israeli city, with most of its former Palestinian inhabitants scattered throughout the world. Najib died on 30 March 1948, just months before the Nakba (catastrophe), the mass expulsion and dispossession of the Arabs of Palestine in 1948 upon the establishment of Israel. Perhaps he was fortunate to be spared that most tragic period in the history of his country. His son, wife, siblings and every one of our common relatives were forced out of Haifa, losing all their property. They did not realise that they would never be allowed to return to their homes and so did not take their personal belongings with them. Furniture, books, manuscripts, memorabilia, family photographs, heirlooms and even personal effects were left behind and never returned. Everything that belonged to them, everything that told their individual stories, was either stolen or seized and deposited in Israeli archives for use by Israeli researchers seeking to understand the history and character of the Arabs whom they were colonising.

A further difficulty was that many of the villages and encampments in which Najib found refuge had also been reduced to rubble, as I discovered when I went in search of them in the hills of the Galilee. I had to scan the terrain with an archaeologist's eye to determine where they had once stood. It was therefore a strange and yet a typically Palestinian quest. Strange because I had to rely heavily on my imagination and train myself to see what was not readily visible. Typical because the process I had to follow to uncover the history of a member of my family is similar to that followed by many Palestinians who had family in the part of Mandatory Palestine that became Israel. I have been able to find only one official Israeli map where all the Palestinian villages existing before 1948 are shown. Next to many of those appears the sinister Hebrew word *harous* (destroyed).

*

Najib was born in 1865. For the first decade of his adult life he had tried his hand at a number of professions, as assistant pharmacist, farmer and translator. Short and plump, he always wore a tarboosh (fez) that leaned forward towards his face in the manner of Beirut merchants. Unlike his brothers, he was not good at making money. He was always involved in pursuing unpopular causes and could hardly earn enough to sustain his family. In 1913, when he was forty-eight, he confessed in an article that he 'despaired of living a free life under the Ottoman Empire'. This made him decide to emigrate to the United States, as many other members of our family had done. Once he had made that decision, he could 'hardly wait to organise [his] affairs and prepare [him]self for the big move'. He was feeling 'only regret for all the efforts [he] applied to establish [him]self in the country'.

I was perfectly capable of recognising these sentiments. I had trained as a barrister in London, but when I returned to work as a lawyer in the West Bank under Israeli occupation I found no professional satisfaction in a ruined legal system. There is hardly a resident of Palestine today who has not considered the option of emigrating. I know all too many who, once they made that decision, regretted all the time they had wasted living in Palestine. I too went through a period when I felt the Israeli occupation would never end and I would be doomed to a life of humiliation, oppression and lack of civil rights. I seriously considered emigrating before turning to human rights activism and writing alongside my professional legal work. The outbreak of the First Intifada in 1987 gave me hope that things would finally change and I dismissed all thoughts of leaving Palestine.

On 24 July 1908 Sultan Abdulhamid (who reigned from

1876 to 1909) granted his subjects a constitution. This was the same constitution that had first been adopted in 1876. Its introduction was part of the process of Westernisation that had begun during the first half of the eighteenth century, with the aim of saving a decaying empire from collapse by creating one Ottoman nation out of many Ottoman subjects, including Muslims, who could be Turks, Arabs, Albanians, Bosnians and others, Christians, who could be Armenians, Greeks, Arabs and others, and Jews, who could be of various nationalities. It also attempted to stem the imperialist designs of Western powers upon the empire advanced by claims of protection for the non-Muslim communities. Constitutional government was to replace absolutism, uniting Muslims and non-Muslims to form 'the Ottoman Nation', based on principles of freedom, justice and patriotism. However, the newly elected parliament, which first met on 19 March 1877, was short-lived. After holding only two sessions Abdulhamid dismissed it and suspended the constitution. Now the experiment was being tried again.

At first Najib received news of the implementation of the constitution with much scepticism. He was not sure that 'among the people or the civil service there was any readiness to act in accordance with its provisions and allow and safeguard the liberties enshrined in it'. Despite this, he decided 'to pin his hopes on it and to support it'. As matters turned out, he was so impressed that such a revolution could have occurred without bloodshed that he decided to stay in the country and not to emigrate.

The Sultan abolished censorship. As a result the number of newspapers and periodicals published throughout the Ottoman Empire jumped to 350, a third of them new. Political opposition groups were allowed, political prisoners released and the army of spies, numbering 30,000, was disbanded. This revolutionary change, which was not to endure through the years of the First World War, was the work of the Committee of Union and Progress (CUP), a secret association the Young Turks had formed in Salonica, which was then still part of the Ottoman Empire. They were a group of army officers and intellectuals who were in power from 1908 until the end of the First World War. Up to that point most Muslim Ottomans were not averse to the establishment's identification with an Arab past. Abdulhamid had once remarked, 'We [Ottomans] are a *millet* [religious community] that has originated from the Arab *millet* ... just as we took civilisation from the Greeks, Europe has taken it from us.' This identification with the Islamic Arab heritage served to legitimate the Ottoman claim to the caliphate. The shift the CUP brought about in the ideology of the empire from Islam to Turkish nationalism proved detrimental to the future of the entire region. In the decades following the First World War the Middle East was reorganised. Rather than one multi-ethnic empire ruling the whole region, as had been the case for the last 450 years under the Ottomans, it was fragmented into Turkey in Anatolia and a number of small new nation states created by the imperial powers of the day: Iraq, Syria, Lebanon, Jordan and Israel.

As it turned out, Najib was right in his initial misgivings about the future. Nationalism was late in coming, but when it arrived it resulted in the genocide of the Armenian communities in Anatolia in 1915, the forcing out of Greeks from Turkey and of Turks from Greece in 1923, and in 1948 of most of the Christian and Muslim Arabs from Palestine. Wars shatter tranquil worlds. This was how the First World War affected Najib. Until it ended he had insisted on defining himself as 'the Ottoman'. With the intrusion of nationalism, Najib's world was broken apart and restructured.

The years immediately following the implementation of

the constitution were an active time of hope and change. Najib's fortunes improved. In 1908 in Haifa he started the Al Karmil publishing house and newspaper of the same name (which is the Arabic for Mount Carmel), transforming himself from a farmer and translator into a campaigning journalist. But the start of the First World War significantly complicated matters for him. As a public figure and editor of a major newspaper, his views on the impending war were known. He expressed them in numerous articles published in his newspaper. Perhaps this was the problem. As Najib was English-educated and Christian, it was only natural for the Ottoman authorities to assume that he would give his allegiance to the Allies and perhaps even cooperate with them in their war efforts against the Axis powers. The Germans knew he was opposed to Ottoman participation in the war on their side. Someone like Najib was dangerous at a time when propaganda was an important weapon in the war. They wanted him on their side. Or, if this was not possible, they wanted him silenced.

In his autobiographical novel, *Mufleh al Ghassani*, penned at the beginning of the British Mandate in Palestine, Najib describes in precise detail his movements during the years when he was on the run from the Ottoman police: the people he met, who gave him refuge and what he did throughout those three difficult years. As such it provided me with a wealth of information on which the account in this book is based. There is hardly any mention of his wife and children, but perhaps that is no wonder, as she ran away with an Ottoman soldier. Nor for that matter do women figure much in the book. Not only was it a world of men in which Najib moved, but there is never any mention of how he felt, never any complaint about the hardships he had to endure. Stoics seem to make bad novelists. And perhaps most annoyingly for me, he moves through the glorious countryside of the Galilee, but there is never any description of the landscape. Even with my anti-colonial sentiments, I came to appreciate T. E. Lawrence, with his great capacity for seeing and describing the landscape in which he moved and prefer reading him to reading my unseeing great-great-uncle.

Ned Lawrence, who would eventually become known to the world as 'Lawrence of Arabia', was described by a contemporary as having 'a very keen face. You could see the pressure behind it.' He had fair hair and electric blue eyes – everyone always noticed his eyes. Too short to be a regular army officer, in 1914 he began working as an intelligence officer in Egypt. Before that he spent a summer touring on foot the chain of citadels build by the French seven centuries earlier to defend what is today Lebanon and western Syria. France's determination to return to Syria was an ambition he was determined to thwart. The tribesmen he met on his travels he later recruited to help the British in their efforts against the Ottoman forces in the First World War. But it was not just the Ottomans that Lawrence hoped to remove: with Sharif Hussein of the Hijaz as figurehead, he believed they could 'rush right to Damascus and biff the French out of all hope of Syria'. Thanks to a series of important postings he held during and after the war, he was able to play a crucial role in the formulation of British policies in the region.

In Najib's account there is not a single admission throughout the three exacting years he spent on the run of being sick or feeling tired. The only time he complains is when he had to endure lice during the last stage of his escape on the eastern side of the River Jordan, while living as a shepherd with the Bedouins in the wilderness and sleeping with the goats. From tracing his life and reading his works, I developed a deep empathy with and appreciation of my great-great-uncle, but I disliked his novelistic account, which

I found poorly written. Clearly the man was dedicated to the cause he espoused but had no talent for novel writing.

He describes two encounters that took place before his country's participation in the war. The first was with the German director of the railway in Haifa. The line from Haifa to Dera'a, a northern village in what is now Jordan, had been completed in 1905 as an addition to the main Hijaz Pilgrim Railway, which ran from Damascus to Medina in the Hijaz, in the south-western part of the Arabian peninsula. The director asked Najib when he thought the Ottomans would enter the war. Najib's answers are blunt, revealing a man who was ready, whatever the personal cost, to speak truth to power. He said that he did not believe that those in government were idiotic enough to participate: 'For many years we've been praying to God to pit the English and the Germans against each other so they would stay off our backs. Are we so crazy as to enter the fray now?' The director answered that he thought Najib was 'more fanatical than the Muslims', to which Najib responded that he was indeed 'fanatical about [his] country and [his] people'.

The second encounter was with the German consul in Haifa. The consul summoned Najib to a meeting and proceeded to boast about Germany, its strength and capabilities. He assured Najib, 'The interest of the Ottomans demands that you support Germany.' To which Najib answered, 'If Germany had a fleet to protect the long coastline of the empire along the eastern Mediterranean Sea I would support joining your side.' The consul told him, 'Mines can protect the coastline just as well,' but Najib was unconvinced.

Reading about this incident, I felt it was more foolhardy than brave for a citizen of a country on the brink of war to speak his mind so openly. But that was Najib's way.

The consul then complained that 'the Muslim Arabs are enamoured of England, the Christian Catholics infatuated with France and the Orthodox with Russia. As to the Protestants they too support England. Germany is loved by no one.'

Najib pointed out that, unlike the English, French and Russians, the Germans had not established missions, schools or hospitals. How, then, could they expect to win anyone's allegiance? 'In any case,' Najib added, 'the support exhibited by the various sects to the French, English and Russians only demonstrates these people's fidelity. So if Germany worked at protecting the Arabs from the oppression which the Unionist government is inflicting on them, their hearts would be full of admiration and support for Germany.'

Najib believed that it was German pressure that led the Ottoman government to adopt, prior to the start of the war, a policy antagonistic to the Arabs. Widespread arrests and hangings of Arab leaders were taking place more frequently than ever before. He argued in his newspaper that such oppressive policies had never been pursued in past wars by the Ottomans and blamed Germany for encouraging the Unionist government to pursue them now. He argued that this was causing deep divisions between Arabs and Turks.

As recounted in his novel, only at this point in the encounter did it become clear that the German consul was attempting to recruit Najib as a propagandist for the German cause. The consul tells Najib, 'The love of Catholics for the French runs deep in their veins. It cannot be wrested out of them without bloodshed. As to the other denominations the time for working with them to win their allegiance has passed. We are in the eleventh hour. Do you understand what I'm saying? If you support Germany you will be rewarded with the assistance and payment we spoke about.' Najib claims that in response to this appeal for his collaboration he told the consul that the only way for Germany to win the hearts of the people was by changing its policy.

In late October 1914 the Ottomans entered the war on the side of the Germans. By then the war had been raging for some months and the devastation it would cause had already become evident. On the night of 2 March 1915 Najib's brother Rashid, the pharmacist, who lived on Mount Carmel in Haifa, heard a knock on his door. He was expecting the Ottoman police to come and arrest him. Times were unsettled and hordes of people had been rounded up and either sent into exile or taken to Damascus for a brief military trial, after which many had been hanged.

Rashid opened the door a crack, asking, 'Who is it?'

'Open up,' said a voice Rashid recognised as the town priest's.

'What brings you here at this unholy hour? Aren't you afraid to be out with all the patrols and spies who never sleep? These days even the walls have ears. Come in. Come in.'

The priest had come, he said, to advise Rashid to send his brother Najib away from Haifa.

'Why?' asked Rashid.

'Because Fakhri Pasha in Damascus has been enquiring about him and his political leanings. This is a time of war. A dangerous time, when even decent government officials are afraid to tell the truth for fear that they themselves will come under suspicion.'

'But where should he go?' asked Rashid. 'Isn't it better to stay where he is known, where government officials know him and would defend him against any accusation? If he flees it would raise suspicion that he is indeed guilty.'

'Had the government officials been able to protect him, the highest ranking among them would not have commissioned me to relay this advice to you. People are in a state of panic. Everyone is thinking: I have to preserve my own life and you can do what you want with the others.'

In his autobiographical novel Najib writes that his brother Rashid could not sleep that night. He could hardly wait for the curfew to end. At daybreak he left his house and rode into the centre of town, where Najib lived, in order to warn him. It was a clear wintry morning, the air crisp and still. Down below he could see the heartening view of the sky-blue Mediterranean stretching out across the bay of Haifa.

Najib describes himself as having been a constant source of trouble for the family and gives voice to his brother's complaints about repeatedly needing to try to keep him in check. As I read his rueful description, I thought of my own brother Samer. More than any of my other siblings, he takes after the Nassars. He has that same deep, sonorous voice and wonderfully dry humour. He must have felt the same way Rashid did after my mother called him that night when she heard of the order for my arrest. Without hesitation he came over and, like Najib and his brother, we discussed what to do. Did Samer leave my house that night feeling burdened by my refusal to renounce activism and raise a family of my own, as he was doing?

Najib was surprised to see his brother this early in the morning, saying, 'It's not like you to come to visit so early in the morning. What brings you here?'

Rashid told his brother what the priest had advised.

Over breakfast the two brothers deliberated. Rashid tried his best to remove from his voice any hint of recrimination or blame. Najib told his brother of an incident two weeks earlier that still caused him anxiety.

'Our old friend Attallah came over and asked me to accompany him because there was something he wanted to talk about. It concerned his son, who had absconded to join the Allies. He said he had received a letter from him, asking for vital information that the Allied army needed. They were

14

thinking of landing troops here and wanted information about the shoreline, the prices of commodities, available vehicles and the number of soldiers stationed nearby. Attallah asked me whether I would be willing to take the letter and go with him to the Anglican Church, where we could read it in peace and think of the right response. I asked him why he would not carry the letter himself. He said he was afraid. When he said this,' Najib recounted, 'my suspicions that I was being framed were raised, especially as the place to which he had suggested we go to read the letter was not far from the house of the German consul. So I answered, "What have we to do with such matters? We are no experts who can give such information. I suggest that if you have such a letter you immediately destroy it, because having it on you will constitute a danger to your life." I didn't want Attallah to suspect what I was thinking, so I invited him to come with me to visit a mutual friend. Once there Attallah disappeared momentarily, claiming to have destroyed the letter on his return. Before he left I checked my pockets to make sure he had not slipped it there without my knowledge. I also checked all the places where we had been, but found no trace of the letter. What I suspect is that this "friend" was trying to frame me and deliver me to the German consul on a charge of treason. This way he would have removed any suspicions that the desertion of his son had placed on him.'

As it turned out, this was only one of a number of attempts throughout the course of the war when fellow Christians tried either to frame Najib or to attribute to him blame for the treasonous actions of others.

Rashid now understood the background and became convinced that his brother was in danger of being arrested, put on military trial, charged with treason and hanged.

'You must go into hiding,' he said with real urgency.

They discussed how Najib should set about it and whether

he should leave the country and go into exile. Najib was concerned about his family, his young wife, two sons and daughter.

'Should I take them with me?' he asked his brother.

'No. Leave them in Haifa. I will take care of them,' Rashid promised.

His brother wanted him to move away from the areas under Ottoman control and, as many exiles had done, flee to Egypt, where the British were in control. But Najib refused. He feared that if it became known that he had gone abroad the authorities would assume that he had joined the enemy and this would put his family in danger. It was best to stay in the country but remain out of sight. For the time being they resolved that the wisest course of action for him was to leave his home in Haifa and go to live in Nazareth, thirty kilometres to the south-east. So the next day, telling his wife nothing about the danger facing him, Najib simply said that he had business to attend to in Acre in the north. He had to leave immediately but would return the next day or, failing that, the day after.

Compared with other major Palestinian towns – Jerusalem, Jaffa, Nablus and neighbouring Acre – Haifa is a relatively new city. In its present location, its existence began in the mid-eighteenth century when, in 1764, the governor of Acre, Dhahir al 'Umar, laid waste the older hamlet of Haifa al Atiqa, located some two and a half kilometres to the west of the modern site, and transferred the population, numbering around 250 people, to a new location that he had surrounded by a protective wall. He also built a citadel overlooking the settlement to the south, the remains of which were still in use at the time of the British occupation in 1918.

Haifa has been compared to Beirut, with its similar large buildings, glass shopfronts, red-tiled and broad-windowed houses, vibrant life and beautiful natural surroundings. Perhaps that was why the Nassars chose to settle here. Their first impression of the city when they arrived in the last quarter of the nineteenth century from their village of A'yn Anoub in the Lebanese mountains was how clean the paths and alleys were, and how well behaved and educated the people. Here they could lead a proper urban life. They had no doubt that, next to Beirut, Haifa was the most advanced town on the eastern Mediterranean.

The oldest and most densely populated part of modern Haifa in Najib's time was the agglomeration of residences and public buildings clustered between the narrow central stretch of seashore and the mountain slopes west of the bay and east of the Carmel promontory. Residences in this area were almost entirely confined to the centre and flanks of the narrow valleys, Wadi al Nisnas and Wadi al Salib, though a few isolated buildings had sprung up outside these valleys, such as Rashid's house on Mount Carmel.

The shops and bazaars, churches and mosques were located in the centre of the city and along the northern seashore. Like most Palestinian cities, Haifa also had a major street called Jaffa Road. Jaffa was the Mecca of Palestine to which all roads led, much like ancient Rome. In Haifa, Jaffa Road was the town's principal artery, originally connecting the eastern and western gates. This was also the main market street, divided into sections, each housing a specialised trade. It was by following this road that Najib fled the city. The covered marketplace he passed had been cleaned just before the start of the war, its roof repaired, its alleyways paved with tile.

Further east along the seashore were to be found the oldest public buildings: the post office and government house, which was locally referred to as the *saray* (Persian for house). The small mosque, the public slaughterhouse and prison built from the remains of a Crusader castle were also in this central area, following the coast in both directions. The area functioned as the buffer zone between the residential sectors of the town – the eastern and western quarters. Muslim, Christian and Jewish communities lived in their respective quarters, which were rigidly adhered to in the nineteenth century while sharing the same marketplace and public facilities. In earlier times the traditional quarters had been squeezed between the mountain and the sea and had converged on the shoreline.

New buildings spread southwards to the flanks of Mount Carmel and even to the mountaintop. Initially it was the European, urban immigrant community who bought land and built on the mountain outskirts. The local population then began to follow suit, though on a much smaller scale. The more affluent, like Rashid, built homes on the slopes of Mount Carmel, but Najib could not afford that and lived with his family in Wadi al Nisnas, not far from the old pier built by the Russians in 1905. Here Mount Carmel was closer to the sea and less steep. The town was altogether smaller yet quite attractive. A good place to live.

In the 1890s a French company had won a concession to run a railway line from Damascus to Beirut. This was completed in 1898, depriving Haifa of some of the traffic in grain from the Hauran plain. But when in 1905 the railway line to Dera'a and Damascus was completed, Haifa regained its importance as a port for the export of wheat and barley from the Syrian interior. A large new central railway station was built to handle the traffic and the old pier was extended. The Damascus–Haifa line, incorporated into the Hijaz railway network, was designed to divert economic benefits to the southern shores of the eastern Mediterranean. It was also a way of undermining the importance of Beirut, with its growing local nationalist aspirations and domination by European powers. Both projects, the pier and the railway, had important repercussions on the town's development. In particular the employment opportunities they created attracted a large labour force, mostly Muslim Arabs, from all parts of Palestine as well as from neighbouring Syria and Egypt.

On the flanks of Mount Carmel stood the *burj* (citadel), commanding a bird's-eye view of the central town. Directly below it lay the religious centres of the Christians, Jews and Muslims. To one side spread Harat al Kana'is (the church quarter), where the Maronite, Greek Catholic, Greek Orthodox and Latin churches were congregated. The Great Mosque, with its spacious public forecourt, was nearby. That clear sunny morning in March 1915 Najib's broad-shouldered, imposing figure could be seen crossing Jraineh Square in front of the Great Mosque and going to Sahat al Arabat (the transport centre), where he hired a horse-drawn carriage to take him south to Nazareth.

Nazareth seems an odd choice for a city to hide from the Ottoman authorities, for this was where the leader of the army squadron resided. In fleeing there, Najib was coming to the regional seat of power rather than running away from it. But then he had good relations with Ottoman officials and wanted to consult them on what he should do. In the novelised account of his escape, on which I relied heavily in tracing his escape route, Najib makes no secret of his unshakeable allegiance to the empire and the good relations he had with its officials. Today the prevailing popular view among Arabs is that the four centuries of Ottoman rule comprise our Dark Ages. Except for recent revisionist accounts, history books have nothing good to say about that time or the long-surviving empire. Its waning years were the war years, marked by famine and pestilence. Conscription into the Ottoman army meant almost certain death. These were the terrible memories that persisted in people's consciousness for many decades, the way such experiences do. Four centuries were judged by the last four years. This was why, when a recent edition of *Mufleh al Ghassani* was published in Haifa, the publisher found it necessary to include an introduction that justified Najib's favourable views of the Ottoman authorities. Sixty years after his death, Najib's views remain controversial.

Yet he was not alone. His colleagues at Al Muntada al Arabi, a literary society that advocated improving the conditions of Arabs within the Ottoman Empire, did not consider themselves enemies of the Ottomans or desire the defeat of the Sultan. Even though he was a Christian in a Muslim state headed by a Sultan claiming to be the Caliph of the Muslims, Najib believed that it was possible for the three 'Religions of the Book' to coexist and live freely within the Ottoman system he sought to perpetuate. His call was reformist in nature and not based on religion. As a Christian he did not seek to separate from the Muslim Ottomans. He wanted decentralisation and a greater measure of autonomy for the Arabs, who to his mind included Muslims, Christians and Jews, all of them Ottoman citizens belonging to different *millets*. He could not have conceived of the fragmentation of the region into the mosaic of countries that it would become. How different this seems from the way the conflict is perceived today, as a struggle mainly between Israeli Jews and Muslim Arabs.

Najib had always thought of himself as a loyal Ottoman citizen. He had expressed this position in his articles in *Al Karmil*. He knew reform was needed and advocated strong Arab independence, but within the Ottoman structure. His main concern was what would happen to his country if the Ottomans were no longer there to protect it from the onslaught of the colonialists and in particular the Zionists, whose plans for Palestine he was more familiar with than most. To him the true fight was against colonialism. Whether victory in the Great War went to the British or the Germans, the collapse of the Ottoman Empire would open the gates for the colonisation of the Levant. The Ottoman regime might need reforming but it was a multi-ethnic system that never attempted to colonise the land.

Unlike Hussein Ibn Ali, the Sharif of Mecca, who in June 1916 started the Arab Revolt in the Hijaz with British support, Najib's struggle was not against the Ottomans. He did not want the empire destroyed and many of his contemporaries must have held similar views. But to state this publicly, as Najib did after the collapse of the empire, when there was a growing belief among Arabs that it was the Ottomans who had brought ruin to them with their 450-year-long rule, was an act of both courage and foresight. Just as he had been among the first to recognise the danger Zionism posed to the Arabs of Palestine, so he was one of the first to appreciate the virtues of the Ottoman system.

Najib was a trusting character and perhaps naively placed unwavering confidence in the Ottoman regime. After leaving his wife and children in Haifa and coming to hide in Nazareth, the first thing he did was to call on two Ottoman officials. The first was Sabih Nasha'at, the Iraqi general who led the Ottoman squadron stationed in Nazareth. For a couple of hours the two men discussed the prevailing situation. They had different views on what constituted the graver danger. Najib was more concerned about the Zionist onslaught and how it was likely to benefit from the war. Nasha'at was more worried about German colonisation should Germany be victorious. Najib tried to sum up the issue thus: 'To a large extent we now have self-rule. The hand clutching our throat might be coarse but it is not an iron grip. This is because it is weak and has an eastern character. If we should be gripped by a European hand it will surely be bronze even if it wore a silk glove.'

After leaving the general, Najib went to see Fawzi Malki, the *qaim makam* (district commissioner) of Nazareth. He then went to have lunch with his friend Nameh Safouri at the Victoria Hotel, before taking his afternoon nap. Reading this, I marvelled at the similarity between us. Even in the worst of times Najib would not miss his nap, just as I am loath to miss a meal.

He was awakened by knocking on his door. It was the Anglican priest, Salah Saba, who had just been to Haifa. He looked perturbed. When Najib asked what was happening, the priest seemed reluctant to speak. Najib grew impatient.

'Tell me the news,' he said. 'I can take it.'

'The gendarmerie have just been to your brother's house. They searched it and arrested Rashid. They also searched the homes of your other relatives and sent a telegram to Acre asking for you.'

'And what have they done to Rashid?'

'They said they wanted to banish him to Damascus with others. As for you, they want you to appear before the military court.'

'What do you suggest I do?'

'Go into hiding,' said the priest emphatically.

'But wouldn't it raise suspicion if I went into hiding?'

'You must do it while we try to find out what they want from you.'

Before he could decide on taking such a big step Najib felt he still needed more advice. He went to the house of his friend the venerable Sheikh Wajih Zaid Kilani, a well-known dignitary held in high esteem by the Ottoman authorities.

The sheikh told him that the order of the day was chaos: 'Periods of transition to a state of war are always a source of worry. The transfer of power from the hands of civilian and judicial administrators to those of military men only leads to chaos. Leaders become so drunk with power that they relish senseless assaults, seizing every opportunity to avenge themselves against those who dare to criticise them. The mere word of an informer or spy is enough to have them do away with the life of the innocent. It is as though governments at war are consumed by fire.'

I know about this all too well. My father was a victim of the chaos that prevailed in the West Bank in the mid-1980s before the First Intifada.

The sheikh continued, 'Under these circumstances prudence dictates that if you know that someone has informed on you, you must do all you can to avoid falling into the hands of the military. I advise you to go into hiding while we try to find out why the government is really after you. And stay in hiding until the fire is extinguished and it becomes possible circumspectly to inform those responsible of the truth about you.'

Najib listened intently. He was now convinced that he must not give himself up. He had to go into hiding. Once he had made the decision, he began to feel that all eyes were upon him. I know that feeling also. In its early days the offices of the human rights organisation I had helped establish, Al Haq, were stormed by the Israeli army. After that they kept us under surveillance. On one occasion I went into the office to smuggle out some files and as I walked into the street with them I felt that everyone was looking at me. It was the same street I had walked along thousands of times during my life in Ramallah. I knew every one of the shopkeepers along the way. Yet that morning everything appeared disconcertingly different as I walked, fearing that there were spies watching me, preparing to report my every move to the Israeli military authorities.

Najib waited until after dark before moving into the home of a close friend, Kamel Kawar, who had a wife and two sons. There he was given a room that was kept closed to everyone except members of the household. He describes Kawar as a descendant of the Ghassanids, one of two Christian Arab tribes living in the Syrian countryside before the Islamic conquest who did not convert to Islam. Perhaps this was why he called the main character of the novelistic account of his escape Mufleh, a good Arab name meaning the successful one, and Al Ghassani, in reference to the Ghassanids.

The Ghassanids came from Yemen and for a time dominated the Syrian countryside. Their main base was in Busra, but they also had another one in the Golan Heights, the Syrian territory under Israeli occupation since June 1967. They had been commissioned by the superpower of the day, the Roman Empire, to protect the borders from marauders such as the Bedouins and other invaders. Despite the domination of the land for many centuries by Muslim rulers, Christian Arabs survived and still have notable families like the Kawars, who trace their lineage to that ancient mini-power that now only historians remember.

Najib planned to stay two weeks with the Kawars to plan his next move. No one knew his hiding place except the owners of the house, his friend Sheikh Wajih Zaid and Najib's own brothers. But news travels fast and he began to get visitors.

When Najib was alone he devoted himself to writing. He was working on two novellas which, once they were finished, he gave to his brother to store in a tin can that could be buried in the garden and retrieved once the war was over. But his brother later destroyed them for fear that the invading British forces might find them and prosecute him. Then he began a book on dry farm agriculture that he based on his readings about the subject and his own experiences. This was another way in which I felt an affinity to my great-great uncle: we both shared an interest in agriculture. His last years were spent between Haifa and Beisan, where he had a banana farm. He believed that the scarcity of water in the country made it important for farmers to know about methods of cultivation that required minimal amounts of water. In this Najib was ahead of his time. He was thinking of developing the kind of agriculture suited to a country that suffered from scarcity of water while the early Zionists were going the other way. They were preparing schemes for water-intensive farming, for which they needed to control the water sources. With the creation of Israel, these would become the hallmark of a state that, in pursuing policies based on then popular notions of controlling nature rather than living in harmony with it, would create endemic water shortages in the country.

Najib was sure he would not be able to stay long at his friend's house. Once the Ottomans joined the war, food became scarce and the authorities began conscripting able-bodied young men. Until 1908 Christians had been spared military service, but that year the exemption was lifted. This meant that both Kamel and his elder son were eligible for the draft. The family lived in dread of the men being taken away. Both had to leave the house every time they suspected the authorities were coming for them. To harbour a wanted man was dangerous and Najib had no wish to add to the family's burden.

As it was impossible to remain there without exposing his friend to danger from the military authorities, he decided to leave and rented a garden shed in the grounds next to the Austrian Hospital. Nearby was a *jubkhana* (Turkish for an

arms depot) guarded by soldiers headed by Abu Faris, a lieutenant from Aleppo. One day the Austrian director of the
hospital complained to the head of the squadron that the
soldiers guarding the *jubkhana* were stealing his almonds.
Abu Faris was called in and warned, so that night he and his
men stayed up. Around midnight they heard rustling in the
trees.

Abu Faris pointed his gun in that direction and shouted,
'To the ground or I'll shoot.'

A man stood there, frozen with fear. Abu Faris went up to
him and saw it was Abu Sharra', the man who sold vegetables
that he brought on his donkey from the village of Saffuriya.
Abu Faris threw him to the ground and proceeded to beat
him.

The man screamed, 'Leave me alone and I'll give you a
valuable bit of information.'

Abu Faris ordered his men to tie him down and leave.
When they had all gone, he asked the man for the promised
intelligence.

Abu Sharra' blabbed, 'Over there in the garden shed not
far from here is a political man, a fugitive, wanted by Jamal
Pasha. In the morning I will lead you to him and you will be
paid handsomely for capturing him.'

Next morning Najib was still asleep when he heard a
knock on the door. He rose from his bed, overcome with fear.
But he controlled his voice and asked quietly, 'Who is it?'

Abu Faris shouted, 'Open up.'

Najib put his *abba* (the long, dark-coloured loose robe
traditionally worn by Arab men) over his shoulders and
opened the door to see a tall, imposing soldier filling the
whole frame.

'Please come in,' said Najib, looking straight at the officer
with his bright brown eyes.

'Would you like to come and visit me? I'm the lieutenant of the *jubkhana*.'

'First will you have a cup of coffee with me?'

'Why not? I will even have breakfast with you and then you'll come to visit me at your leisure.'

The two breakfasted and became friends, and Najib was pleased with this new contact, who might be of help to him in the future.

The day after, Abu Faris arranged for someone to take the donkey belonging to Abu Sharra'. When Abu Sharra' came looking for it, Abu Faris told him, 'Even though you implicated me in stealing almonds from one of our allies, the Austrians, I'll help you find your donkey. But I have one condition. After we find your donkey you will leave Nazareth and never show your face here again.'

After this Abu Faris continued to visit Najib and when there was a search in the neighbourhood Najib would go to the *jubkhana* to hide until the raid was over.

Najib had that open, generous nature which made him endearing. Throughout his long escape he always managed to find those who would feed and hide him even at risk to their own lives. In his character and sociability Najib was more like my brother and father than me. I expend a lot of my energy guarding my privacy. Not so Najib. He was not someone who cared about money or material comforts. He was generous with his time and would do anything for his friends, and in return they would do anything for him. But unlike my brother Samer, who is not embittered, Najib's life would end in disappointment.

One of those who came to visit Najib around this time was Salim al Ahmad Abdulhadi of Jenin (the nearby town now in the Israeli-occupied West Bank), a member of the Decentralisation Party, which advocated autonomy for Arabs within the Ottoman Empire. He had come to Nazareth on his way to Aley, in the Lebanese mountains, to stand military trial on trumped-up charges. He was brought to visit Najib by Abdullah Mukhlis, who had bailed him out. Najib asked Salim whether the soldier in charge of delivering him to the court would agree to cooperate in his escape. Salim answered that he would agree to anything.

'Then,' said Najib, 'after Abdullah hands you over, you leave Haifa as quickly as you can.'

'And go where?'

'Hide with one of our friends until we find out how things are going.'

'I cannot risk exposing my family to persecution. Anyway, I have many Ottoman friends who respect me and will surely stand up for me.'

Najib continued to insist. 'We'll be together,' he said. 'You must not risk going to the mock military trial.'

But his friend said, 'Save your energy. I have made up my mind.'

Najib risked leaving Nazareth from time to time to see his family. He had grown a beard and he wore peasant clothing as a disguise. This must have been how he looked when he visited his brother Ibrahim, my grandmother Julia's father, at the Nassar Hotel in Haifa's Street of the Kings. It was this image that had stayed with her. Many years later in Ramallah she described how she failed to recognise her uncle, taking him for a beggar knocking at the door asking for alms. She also said he had lost a lot of weight. Eating good food was central to my grandmother's life and she felt sorry for him. At least in Nazareth he was staying in relative comfort.

But soon after matters worsened. With the failure of the February 1915 attack on the Suez Canal by the Axis powers, in which many Arab conscripts perished, Arab discontent with the war increased. The policy of hanging Arab leaders on the flimsiest of evidence did not help. They felt they were being sacrificed for a war in which they did not believe. To quell the rising rebellion against the war, Jamal Pasha instituted a reign of terror. He called for expediting the trials taking place in Damascus and Aley of the members of the Ottoman Decentralisation Party and the members and president of Al Muntada al Arabi, to which Najib belonged. All of them were found guilty and sentenced to death. They were hanged in the central square in Beirut, which came to be known as Sahat al Shuhada (Martyrs' Square). Their bodies were left hanging for weeks, clad in white djellabas fluttering with the wind, with flies swarming all over their bent and broken necks.

Najib's friend Salim al Ahmad Abdulhadi was hanged on the morning of 21 August 1915 after a brief military show trial. The news of his death profoundly shocked Najib and he decided he must leave Nazareth. He asked his friend Sheikh Mahmoud Tabari (so called after Tiberias, which in Arabic is Tabariah) for a horse and was given a sturdy steed.

His plan was to ride first to Tiberias. The route took him through the towns of Ableen and Hittin, passing through A'yn Mahel. Hittin, eight kilometres north-west of Tiberias, was a particularly attractive village with breathtaking views. Its houses stood on descending terraces. Built of stone, with roofs made of arched wood, these dwellings were surrounded by orchards. Nearby was the grave of Nabi Shu'ayb, the holy prophet of the Palestinian Druze community, who identify him with Jethro, Moses's father-in-law. Najib intended to stay in Tiberias for a few days at a friend's house before moving on. And so began his flight, which lasted for another two years and two months, in the course of which he moved through the Lower Galilee region, crossed the River Jordan and spent time disguised as a shepherd on the eastern bank of the river.

It was this trek that I was determined to reproduce, exploring the route on foot wherever possible. And this is what I was thinking about on the night of 18 September 1996 as I waited for the knock on the door, not knowing that thanks to the intercession of friends – and the promise I subsequently made to appear next day before the Palestinian prosecutor – I would be spared the humiliation of arrest and incarceration.

2

The View from Mount Arbel

The hill on which my wife, Penny, and I were standing on that clear, crisp day at the end of 1996 is called Mount Arbel. It is one of the highest points on the plateau of Galilee. Below me I could see all too clearly the new geography of the land stretching out before me. The arable land was very neatly parcelled up and cultivated, most of it now in the hands of Israeli Jews. Here and there were the mainly Jewish villages, so well defined, so carefully planned. The land was like a mosaic of different parts all carefully put together, sometimes manicured, with well-defined edges. I had come here to try to imagine how the area must have looked at the time of Najib Nassar.

From this precipitous cliff in what might be described as a wide trough surrounded by high hills, I could observe the beautiful sweep of the Great Rift Valley encompassing Lake Tiberias and stretching beyond it northwards into Lebanon. In the distance was Mount Hermon, which in Arabic is called

Jabal al Sheikh because of the resemblance between its snow-capped top and the white turban worn by sheikhs (headmen). This was a good spot from which to get a sense of the flow of the Rift Valley, which extends from the Taurus Mountains in southern Turkey to Mozambique in East Africa. Viewing this relatively small stretch, one could still observe how the valley's basin contains lakes and rivers surrounded on both sides by higher ground, creating what in some areas resembles rock walls. One geologist has compared the process of rifting to the fracturing of an arch that has been pulled apart by tension so that the keystone drops. Other geological changes resulting from volcanic eruptions account for the formation of the terrain here. The volcano Hittin erupted between 4 and 4.5 million years ago. The surrounding land is full of volcanic rocks and solidified lava in the form of basalt. Not far from where the Arab village of Hittin once stood there is evidence of faulting responsible for the dramatic split between the rock hill on which I was standing and the one just north of it, between which lies Wadi al Hamam.

Here is how T. E. Lawrence described the area in a letter he wrote to his mother in 1909: 'The plain is very fertile and very highly cultivated, and the lake gives abundance of water: it is the best place I have found yet in Palestine. Imagine walking on a grass path (real grass green) by the water's edge through oleander shrubs, which sometimes meet above one's head, and were all in bloom: the actual beach, where the grass does not grow in the water, is of a beautiful white sand – altogether charming.' He goes on to describe Tiberias as 'one of the most Romanised provinces of Palestine'.

But this morning, when I walked along some of the same paths that Lawrence trod a century earlier to reach this cliff, I saw no Roman ruins. In 1948 the Israeli army destroyed many of the archaeological sites in and around the city. It was different during Najib's time. Lawrence writes: 'Everywhere one finds remains of splendid Roman roads and houses and public buildings.' Most of the land I passed was farmed by Israeli Jews. I was struck by how they watered the olive trees, which in our hills in the West Bank get no water most of the year. The absence of Arab farms would have pleased the Englishman, for whom the best times were those when Palestine was under Roman rule. Then 'the country was well peopled and well watered artificially: there were not 20 miles of thistles behind Capernaum! And on the way round the lake they did not come upon dirty, dilapidated Bedouin tents, with the people calling to them to come in and talk, while miserable curs came snapping at their heels.'

In 1948, as part of Operation Palm Tree, the Israeli army forced the Palestinians out of most of the villages and Bedouin encampments around Nazareth, confiscating the majority of the cultivated land of those who managed to stay. I passed only one Arab farm this morning while climbing to this high spot. I didn't know the owners but marvelled at their heroic success in surviving the war and the confiscations that followed. This Arab farm was immediately distinguishable from the more mechanised larger farms around it. It had life – smells and sounds. You knew you were passing a farm. You smelt the smoke of their *taboun* oven. You heard the loud voices of the mothers calling their children and the crowing of the cock asserting his presence and, yes, the annoying semi-wild dog that pursued you, barking all the way. Somewhere nearby was the railway station where the train arriving from Damascus stopped on its way to Haifa. From here to Damascus it could not have taken longer than two hours by train.

Before ending his letter to his mother, Lawrence laments the demise of Roman rule, when 'Palestine was a decent country'. Looking ahead to a future which, as it turned out, he had a crucial role in forging, he writes: 'it could so easily be made so again. The sooner the Jews farm it all the better: their colonies are bright spots in a desert.'

It was precisely these 'bright spots' that worried Najib. In a piece that he published a few years later in his newspaper, *Al Karmil*, describing what he had seen on the plain of Marj Ibn Amer (plain of Esdraelon) while looking down from the village of Al Mattal, not far from where I was standing, my great-great uncle wrote: 'Before me lay the Jewish colonies with their red-tiled roofs encrusting the plain facing the sombre dark colours of the Arab villages like colonial banners spread by the British. I was reminded of the confrontation between the dark magnanimous faces of the Arabs and the glittering helmets and armour of the Roman and Crusader warriors. In earlier times this plain has been the stage for many fierce battles between nations and ideologies.' Looking ahead, he predicted more 'dangers and horrors for this ravaged country where religion, colonialism and capitalism will cause violent clashes in this very plain'.

In many of the articles Najib wrote prior to the start of the Great War he blamed the large landowners for mismanaging their farms and impoverishing the sharecroppers who did the work for them. The rate at which these landowners were selling off their land alarmed him. In 1911 he published a book entitled *Zionism: Its History, Aims and Importance*, in which he informed his readers that the Zionist movement was built on a racial base, with aims both national and political. He demonstrated that Zionism aimed at gaining 'mastery over our country and the sources of our livelihood'. In many ways Najib's struggle to save the land was similar to mine, despite the changed political realities that have occurred in the intervening century. Looking down from Mount Arbel, I could see that Najib's predictions had come true. Only from photographs do I know the landscape as it had been, with Arab villages nestled among the slopes of the beautiful hills. My direct experience of the land is confined to what it has become, now that most Palestinians have been forced to flee.

Unlike Najib, I cannot look from this high cliff and see myself beyond the present borders. My field of vision stops at the Golan Heights, at the border between Israel and Syria that I've never been able to cross, and as matters stand never will. When I go to visit A'yn Anoub, Najib's village in the Lebanese mountains, as I intend to, I will not be able to take the short route that the Nassars did when they relocated to Haifa in the last quarter of the nineteenth century. I'll first have to travel east to Jordan in order to go north-west to Lebanon. They didn't have to cross any border, while I'll have to cross three. Before the First World War, when Najib lived in this area, the whole region was under Ottoman rule. The entire stretch of the Rift Valley, from the Taurus Mountains in the north all the way down to the tip of the Hijaz, modern-day Saudi Arabia, was under one regime. Najib might have had other problems to contend with, but they did not include the fragmentation of the land and the tormenting restrictions on movement that plague my life and the lives of most Palestinians, many Arabs and to a lesser extent Israeli Jews in the Middle East.

Standing on Mount Arbel, I could see the Marj Ibn Amer plain spread out before me like a huge stage, the site of numerous battles that had brought to an end many a long-surviving empire. Crusaders marched across it carrying their colourful banners – black, green and red crosses on white fabric ever more faded with time; Islamic fighters advanced bearing the crescent, their helmets glinting in the sun; and more recently, during the First World War, black hordes of locusts invaded, munching at everything green, bringing famine to the people of the land.

To the north-west I could see the hill with two protruding mounds emerging from the ground. These were the Horns of Hittin, the arena for the decisive battle that took place in 1187 in which Salah al Din (Saladin), the renowned Kurdish-born general and founder of the Ayyubid Dynasty, defeated the Crusader kingdom that ruled from Jerusalem and ended the first 100 years of their command. When I visited the hillside, all that was left of the Palestinian village that had been there was a minaret forlornly shooting out of the thicket concealing the scattered stones that had been used to build the homes of this attractive village, destroyed along with twenty-eight others in the sub-district of Tiberias in 1948 in the course of the Israeli army's operations Hiram and Palm Tree.

South-east of the Sea of Galilee another decisive battle took place on 20 August 636 in a blinding sandstorm between the Emperor of Byzantium, Heraclius, and Muslims led by the second Caliph, Omar Ibn al Khattab. The Christian Byzantines had the larger army but were outmanoeuvred. In the midst of the fighting, the Ghassanid prince and 12,000 Christian Arabs went over to the Arab side. That settled the issue. The Muslim victory was complete and Palestine and Syria lay open to them. Later Heraclius went down to the sea and fled by ship to Constantinople, crying bitterly as he left the shore, 'Farewell, a long farewell to Syria.' In this battle the Christian Arabs were not the only ones to help the Muslims; the Jews also served as their guides.

Further south another important battle took place in 1917, when the Allies won a decisive victory over the Ottoman army, ending their control of the land. The Allies had already defeated the Ottomans in Sinai, the western gateway to the area. They could have contented themselves with expelling the Turks from Sinai and then stood guard at Al Arish, north of the Sinai desert. But it was politically important for them to capture Jerusalem and to do so by Christmas. There was an element of the Crusades here, the Christian West liberating the Holy Land from the infidel Muslims, as there was an element of Christian evangelism in the British government promising that same year in the Balfour Declaration to facilitate the return of Jews to Palestine. The seeds of much that was to come later were sown in that fateful year, which placed the fate of the Arabs squarely in the European orbit after 450 years of Ottoman rule, preventing them from fulfilling their hopes for a united Syria in the Arab Levant and facilitating the creation of Israel as a buffer state between the Arabs in Greater Syria and Egypt, so that there would be no united front on both sides of the Suez Canal. None of this would have happened without the physical conquest by Britain and France of the Levant.

As I surveyed the scene before me, the hills and plains, I knew that this land ought never to be divided. Those living on the Golan Heights look down from their villages at the lake and those living around the lake look up at the Golan Heights and each should be able to visit the other.

This area is so different from the central hills, where I live. The average height of hills here is 300 to 600 metres, although several minor peaks top 900 metres. The steep sides and rocky slopes of the Ramallah hills are replaced by low rounded hills, smooth outlines and grass-covered uplands with an abundance of water from rivers, streams and the singular freshwater lake. The climate is more temperate and humid. Colours and light have a different quality. With the higher levels of humidity in the air, sunlight is not as direct as it tends to be in the central hills and there is more blue here, with the large body of water dominating the scenery.

Like Hittin, many of the Arab villages and Bedouin encampments thriving in Najib's time have been wiped out and new Israeli villages established where they once stood.

The land is now the outcome of a planned vision that has been in the making since the start of the twentieth century, an ideological dream that has been forcibly realised, transforming the land, redividing it, changing farming methods and exploiting every plot available, redistributing it all on an entirely new basis. The transforming process began here, in an area of large plains and plenty of water where gargantuan dreams were possible. Najib was one of the first people to pay attention to what was going on, to try to describe it, warn about its consequences for the Arab community and to document it. This is where the Zionist ideas of the founders of the Jewish state began to take shape, the ideal of return to and 'redemption' of the land, of Jewish labour, of establishing bands of armed guards to protect the Jewish colonies that eventually developed into the Israeli army. The transformation is so immense that if Najib were to visit now he would not recognise the place.

That initial flight from Nazareth on the horse given to him by Sheikh Tabari took Najib in the direction of the village of A'yn Mahel. I wondered whether it was visible from here, and whether those hills I could just make out to the south were the hills of Nazareth. If only there were someone I could ask.

Not far from the only carob tree, near the edge of the cliff in a crevice of sorts, I could see the heads of two men. They looked like they were hiding between the rocks. I didn't suspect they were Arab until some words drifted to my ears. They were deep in conversation. I walked over to their hideout, assuming they must be from the area.

'I wonder whether you could tell me if Nazareth and A'yn Mahel are visible from here?' I asked.

They were surprised to be approached. I was wearing my not-so-clean hiking clothes and carrying my red backpack. Not exactly the way a middle-aged Arab man would kit himself out. And yet I spoke Arabic. They could not be sure who I was.

The older man, whom I learned later is called Basel, eventually answered. 'Nazareth and A'yn Mahel are too far away to be seen from here. They're behind those hills over there. But you can see the Horns of Hittin from here. They're over there, on top of the hill with the two humps.'

As expected, they asked me where I was from. I didn't say Ramallah, wishing to avoid questions of how it was possible with the closure of the West Bank for me to be here. I said, 'Jerusalem.'

'And before that?' Basel asked.

I knew why he asked this. He suspected that I was an Israeli Jew who spoke Arabic. My appearance and the fact that I was with blue-eyed Penny made it unlikely that I was an Arab.

'My family originally comes from Jaffa.'

'Jaffa Tel Aviv or Jaffa Nazareth?'

Now it was my turn. 'Why should you identify Jaffa in reference to Tel Aviv? It is by far the older city.'

'Because there are two Jaffas and you could be referring to either,' Basel explained, somewhat taken aback but still unconvinced that he was not speaking to an Israeli Jew who was perhaps pulling his leg.

I must have sounded like an interrogator when I asked, 'What's the name of the village down there?'

'That's Wadi al Hamam. It's an Arab village and next to it is Migdal, which is Jewish.'

'I wonder why the Israeli army allowed some Palestinian villagers to stay in '48 and forced others to flee?'

'They didn't want to touch the Christians. That's why. Before they left, the British told the Jews they must keep all the Christians and not force them to leave.'

'Surely that is not true. There were Christians in Tiberias

and not a single Arab, whether Muslim or Christian, was allowed to stay. Wadi al Hamam is not a Christian town and yet its inhabitants were allowed to stay.'

But this made no impression on Basel, who seemed to harbour a grudge against Christians. It distressed me to hear this young man distorting history. The more we spoke the more I realised how deeply antagonistic he was to the Christian Palestinians.

'Do you know about Najib Nassar?' I asked him.

'No. Who is he?'

'The editor of *Al Karmil* and one of the first to write about Zionism. He was a Christian. He was a great-great-uncle of mine.'

I felt their discomfort when I confirmed that I was Christian and I found myself feeling annoyed at having to be defensive about the religion into which I was born. I was thinking in particular of Najib. Not that the Israeli leadership did not try to win the Christians to their side, as they had succeeded in doing with the Druze, who practise a religion that is an offshoot of Islam with its own unique features. Under Israeli law they are defined as a distinct ethnic community. The Druze have had a long and complicated relationship with the Israeli state. In 1948 some members of the community fought on the side of the Jewish forces and as a reward their villages, including mixed ones where they lived with fellow Christians and Muslims, were spared the fate of other Arab villages in the area. In certain battles in the Galilee, Druze men fought on either side of the line and ended up killing each other in the course of the conflict. There are many instances when Christian and Muslim families in the region took refuge with Druze families and in this way managed to avoid the fate of others who were forced to flee.

In the summer of 1948 Israeli troops routinely deported

Christians together with the Muslims, but then they started transferring them to transit camps in the central coastal areas. Muslims rarely remained long in these camps but were 'transported' – in the language of the Israeli army – to Lebanon. Christians were now offered a different deal. In return for a vow of allegiance to the Jewish state, they were allowed to return to their villages for a short time. Most Christians refused to participate willingly in such a selective process. As a result, where there were no Druze inhabitants, the army soon meted out the same treatment to Christian and Muslim villages alike. Basel and his friend either did not know this or chose not to acknowledge it.

I also remembered reading that in 1920 Chaim Weizmann, president of the World Zionist Organisation, visited Palestine and held a series of meetings with various Palestinians. He had coffee with Bedouin sheikhs in the Beisan Valley, not far from here. These meetings were arranged by members of the intelligence office of the Elected Assembly, the Zionist body responsible for intelligence and political activities within the Arab population. At the conclusion of his visit he asked the office to draw up a comprehensive plan for countering Arab opposition to Zionism. One of the proposals included 'provocation of dissension between Christians and Muslims'. And here I was, almost a century later, standing on the high hill overlooking Tiberias and having to defend Christians who, just as my own family, had suffered as much as Muslims in their plight as refugees.

Where the Israeli state failed in co-opting the Christian minority left in the country after the Nakba, they succeeded with the Druze, for whom service in the Israeli army is obligatory. I didn't know what experiences the two men might have had with their Christian countrymen that produced such a grudge. Or was it a natural corollary of the new self-image they seemed to have, not so much as Palestinians living in Israel but as Muslims belonging to the vast and growing population of the *ummah* around the world.

'Do you come here often?' I asked.

'Yes. We like it here. It's a short drive from where we live.'

'Where is that?'

'Kufr Cana, the village where Christ changed the water to wine. We get many tourists visiting the church. Did you visit?'

'No, never. And it's my first time here on this mountain. It is so beautiful. One can see the whole area around.'

'It's a good view of the Horns of Hittin. That's why we like to come here, to look at the site of the great battle of Salah al Din when he brought the end of the Crusaders' rule.'

'What do you think was done to the civilians after the defeat of their army?' I mused. 'They could not all have been killed.'

'They left. They took the boats and left. Went back to Europe, where they came from.'

'But they could not have had time to leave. The sea is not so close.'

The other man, who had been silently expressing approval of his friend's assertions, indicated that the Muslims had been kind to Christians. 'Remember Omar and his Covenant. They just had to pay the *jizia* [tax paid by the heretics] and they could stay.'

I thought he was probably thinking that this is what would happen to the non-Muslims of this country once the Islamic state is established. To confirm my hunch I asked, 'Then you believe Muslims will some day take over this land?'

'I'm sure of it,' said Basel's companion. 'Even when I'm driving in the heart of Tel Aviv and looking around me at all these Jews, I keep thinking: These people should not be here and will not be here for long. It is only temporary. When a policeman tries to give me a ticket, I think: Why should he give me a parking ticket? This is my country, not his. I teach this to my three-year-old son. We Palestinians who live here know that the presence of Israel is not going to be for long. They will end up leaving, just like the Crusaders. We know it.'

Not too far away an Israeli teacher in Orthodox clothing was instructing a group of young schoolchildren in a booming voice about the religious significance of this place: the partisans of the Maccabees had hidden in caves just below where we stood. They had sought refuge here and were slaughtered in 161 BCE by the Syrian general Baccides.

Looking at the Israeli children being instructed in the Hebrew history of their country, Basel expressed regret that 'Palestinian schoolchildren were not taken on *tiyuls* like these'. He was not conscious that he had used a Hebrew word for excursion.

Reflecting on the Crusaders' experience in this land, the Israeli sociologist Baruch Kimmerling wrote, 'The Zionists drew a lesson from the demise of the Latin Kingdom. By identifying the major "mistake" of the Christian settlers – their failure to maintain their cultural, technological, and military links with their countries of origin and their openness to the local Levantine culture – the Zionists hope to avoid it.'

Palestinian hatred of Israel and its Zionist policies was hardly new to me. But the extent of the antagonism expressed by these two young men towards those among whom they've lived all their lives I found to be shocking. I had always felt both admiration and envy towards the Palestinians who had managed to stay in their homes in 1948 and wished that my own family had done the same. I considered them the true heroes of the Palestinian struggle. Now for the first time I felt the sense of abandonment they must feel. They had stayed on their land and yet most of it was taken away from them. They are citizens of Israel, a country which by its own definition as a Jewish state excludes them. For years they were considered by fellow Arabs outside Israel as traitors for having stayed behind and taken up Israeli citizenship. As if they had a choice!

I remembered meeting an Israeli Arab lawyer who had a broken nose. When I asked him how he broke it, he told me that he was a boxer: 'When I was young my father told me that to survive in this country you have to fight. So I became a boxer. Then I studied law and became a lawyer, and I haven't stopped fighting.'

Gone is the mix of people that existed in Najib's time. In their place a large variety of Jews from Arab countries, Eastern Europe and from the West, along with those Palestinian Arabs who have managed to stay, now share the land unequally. But gone are most of the Bedouin tribes, Palestinian Arabs and Arabs from various parts of North Africa, and the Marsh Arabs who lived in the Huleh region with their water buffaloes that are now extinct here.

Before leaving I indicated to Basel and his friend that I was a writer and had come here to explore the places where my great-great-uncle Najib Nassar had taken refuge from the Ottoman authorities during the First World War. I didn't want to keep these two young men wondering who I was and why I was here.

As it turned out it was fortunate that I did.

'I have a great-great-grandfather,' Basel told me. 'He was born in 1903.'

'Is he still in good health?'

'Miraculously so.'

'And his memory? How is his memory?'

'Very good. Abu Naif doesn't forget a thing.'

'I'd love to meet him.'

Basel gave me his number. 'I am in my carpentry shop most of the day. You can come there and we'll walk together to the old man's house.'

After passing through Hittin, Najib had stood at the top of a mountain overlooking Tiberias. It could have been this very spot or one nearby. During the twenty-six months that he was on the run, he had hidden south of here. None of that terrain is visible from this high point. This is not why I came here. I came because I wanted to get a panoramic view, a wide-angle perspective of the whole area to help me plan my excursions into Najib's world. I wanted to try to capture a sense of what has happened to the land, how it has changed. To see the route that Najib followed in his great escape, I needed to go south to the hill topped by the Crusader fortress known as Belvoir (French for fine view), near which the Arab village of Kawkab al Hawa once stood. I will do so in the spring, when I plan to visit all the places on Najib's route and meet Abu Naif, Basel's great-great-grandfather in Kufr Cana.

3

Along the River Jordan

It was early in spring several years after my visit to Mount Arbel when Penny and I left Ramallah and travelled north to Tiberias to follow in Najib's footsteps. We could not take the shortest route, through the central hills of Palestine, because it was no longer possible to get to Nablus by car. The three main entrances to the city were blocked by the Israeli army, which required all Palestinians to leave their cars and pass through the checkpoints on foot. We were better off descending to the east first, then driving north along the River Jordan through the Rift Valley and continuing straight on to the Galilee. As we passed through small stretches of fertile land between the hills I saw Israeli army camps usurping the farms. Target-practice ranges were scattered about the countryside, with soldiers training to hunt and kill. Where they camped not a scrap of greenery remained, only the empty cartridges and ruts made by the caterpillar tracks of the heavy Merkava tanks, packing firm the fertile soil of the valley, laying waste the arable land that had once been cultivated.

I felt a great sense of relief every time I was allowed through another of the five checkpoints along the way. As always when travelling during these turbulent times, the persistent worry is that I will be detained at one of these numerous roadblocks and prevented from proceeding with my plans. At some of the army barriers I could see that the soldiers had stopped passengers on a whim, interrogating families because of nothing more than the look of the driver. These days this is called 'ethnic profiling'. Najib was on horseback not far from Nazareth when he was stopped by a group of Ottoman soldiers at a crossroads. I was in my German-made Volkswagen when I escaped detection. As I made my way down between the central hills of the West Bank to the Rift Valley, a depression 260 metres below sea level, I felt like an outlaw, and this profoundly distressed me. A hundred years after Najib escaped the controlling authorities of the day we, the Arab inhabitants, Christian and Muslim alike, have still not stopped running. We are haunted and hunted, made to feel and act like fugitives in our own land.

With all his foresight and sense of foreboding, Najib could not have known the full consequences of the Great War, which he believed the Ottomans should never have entered. He died before he could witness the utter loss of the country and the degradation of its original inhabitants into ghosts, fleeing and concealing themselves as he had had to do during the years he spent in hiding. Nor could he have anticipated the transformation of the landscape from the unique tapestry of numerous small, ancient farming villages belonging to members of the three religions to the large, monochrome, mechanised, Israeli-style farms that have replaced them. When I last visited the Galilee hills where Najib hid, I found no trace of the variety of wild flowers that had once covered the slopes. It seemed that the hills were condemned to the uniformity of green.

No longer did they revel in the splendour of the multitude of colours they wore in the old days, when the farming villages populated them. Like the diversity of human cultures that had once thrived here – the Bedouins and the villagers, the marshland farmers and shepherds coming to Palestine from Egypt, Iran, Jordan, Lebanon, Morocco, a mix of Bahais, Christians, Jews and Muslims – this natural variety has also gone.

During his life Najib used every means at his disposal to save the land from being taken, but to no avail. He was tireless in writing about land sales to Zionist agencies. He tried to educate and intervene. I in turn tried to expose Israel's spurious legal arguments as applied to the territories occupied in 1967. But the opposing forces were much stronger than us. It came down to war, to fighting for the land. Najib died before he could find out how poorly prepared our side was for the conflict that ensued.

In the course of his escape during the first part of the twentieth century, Najib worked with different people from every class, background and level of education – Bedouins, farmers and city dwellers – just as I did when I worked with Al Haq. Like him, I came to appreciate the courage, loyalty and integrity of those who live off the land; and like him, I saw how politics finally destroyed some of them. He witnessed this in the course of the British Mandate in the choices people made – sometimes rationalising the sale of their land to the Zionists and emigrating because they saw no future in the country. I experienced it in the wake of the Oslo Accords and the co-option of people I had trusted.

As we travelled south towards Jericho, I wondered about the consequence of delving into this past. I was beginning to feel it was like settling old scores, attending to deep wounds that refuse to heal. My hope is that I'll succeed in imaginatively recreating the region as it existed at the time of the Ottoman

Empire, when the land was undivided. This will be my way of resisting what Israel has long tried to drill into my head about my place in this ancient land after the fragmentation of our territory by borders, roadblocks, zoning, the building of Jewish settlements and the creation of a new geography that has left me utterly confined. Everything has been designed by Israel to make Palestinians feel like strangers in their own country. Whether it is the huge areas of land expropriated and surrounded by barbed wire that one sees while travelling in most parts of the West Bank, the many settlements, the road signs, the presence of settlers hitchhiking on roads forbidden to Palestinians, the military training areas, the danger and apprehension felt just from using the roads or the uncertainty about being allowed to pass from one part of one's land to another, all these harsh realities conspire to make Palestinians feel that this land is no longer theirs, that it has been claimed by a powerful group who always get their way, so much so that they drive ordinary Palestinians into despair and make them despise life itself.

This means it is so much more important not to relent, not to give way, but to stop and behold the beauty of our land and appreciate what it has to offer. It is the best antidote to the Israeli campaign of despair and alienation. This is why, even though it would delay our arrival, we decided to stop by the side of the road whenever we felt like it and examine the wild flowers in their beauty – the bugloss, the poppies, cyclamens and hollyhocks.

Just before reaching Jericho there is an old sign alerting travellers that they have reached sea level. For many years next to this sign a Bedouin has been offering rides on his camel to tourists, photographing them mounted before the start of their descent to the lowest spot on earth. Just beyond this point the road curves and a small window opens between the hills to reveal the first glimpse of the Dead Sea, calmly nestled in the lowest part of the Rift Valley. The top of this last arid hill of the mysterious Jerusalem wilderness has now been chopped off to widen the ancient road connecting Jericho and Jerusalem, forever doing away with that unique first encounter. The vista of the blue waters now breaks into view rather than sidling through.

Some three kilometres along the road that diverges from the highway and leads to the city stands the new Jericho Intercontinental Hotel, built in 1998, complete with the first casino to be established in the country, the Oasis, which almost led to my imprisonment. In the flat, clay-coloured plain the bulky and sharp-edged structure looks out of place. This was the first modern edifice of such size ever to be built in the area, and it would have been followed by plenty more had the tourist village planned for the vicinity been completed.

There are many incorrigible gamblers among Israelis. Until the Oasis Casino was opened in Jericho, the closest place where they could indulge was Istanbul. Now they could do so by driving the short distance to Jericho and they came in droves. Following its establishment in September 1998, the casino was visited by some 825,000 people, 99 per cent of them Israelis. Every night until the Second Intifada in September 2000, when the casino was closed, it was frequented by a daily average of 2,809 people. They were under the protection of the Palestinian security personnel, who shared the profits with an Austrian corporation, the majority owner of the establishment. Its net profit in 1999 was $54 million. This was the project that got my client into trouble. When he came seeking my legal services I had no idea that powerful people in the Palestinian Authority and Israel's highest political echelons were involved. My client had bid for the land but was kept incarcerated in Jericho until he relinquished his interest in the project. In enterprises of this nature involving high-level politicians from both the Palestinian Authority and Israel the stakes are so high that whoever tries to intervene is struck with all the might available to well-placed politicians. This was but one example of successful cooperation between corrupt politicians on both sides of the divide who forget their political differences as they indulge in Mafia-like operations that bring them huge financial gains. When I tried to intervene on behalf of my client I was brought before the Palestinian prosecutor and forced to forfeit all links with the case. I was only spared further humiliation by the intercession of well-connected acquaintances. However corrupt the Palestinian Authority might have been during its early phase, society was still closely knit enough for personal relations to put some limits on the immoral behaviour to which bad money might otherwise lead.

The crust of the earth is subject to so many tensions and stresses that sometimes it breaks. A fault then develops. Blocks slip off the earth's crust along great ruptures or cracks. Distinctive landforms are associated with faulting: where a succession of tension faults occurs, a series of troughs or rift valleys may result. The Jordan Valley is one such depression. Driving further down into the Rift Valley, we decided to park the car by the side of the road and observe the markers which characterise this amazing geological feature, one of the longest faults on the surface of our planet.

Looking north along the road leading to the valley, it is possible to see hills with strata that had once been parallel to the ground now pointing downwards, providing visual proof of how the land collapsed into itself when this great fault was formed. To my right as we stood by the road was the Dead Sea, which lies like a basin, bordered on either side by sharply cut cliffs and mountains. It is both mysterious and seductive, poetic and lethal, alluring yet treacherous, with many superstitions and fears associated with it. It was once thought to exude noxious fumes that would kill anyone who got too close. And many perished trying to survey and sail it.

In 1915, as Najib was avoiding capture, the Ottoman authorities developed and expanded the Dead Sea Port on the western shores of the sea in an area called Al Jadida, turning it into a military harbour used for transporting grain from east Jordan to the districts west of the River Jordan. Experienced sailors were recruited from among the most able-bodied mariners in the port of Jaffa to work at the Dead Sea Port. In his diaries the musician and diarist Wasif Jawharia describes the ceremonial opening of the port and the musical evening that was held in celebration, at which he performed on the oud (a lute-like string instrument popular for performing Arabic eastern music). Most accounts of the experience of life during the First World War describe the horrors of those years, but Jawharia's is an exception. He writes of euphoric evenings spent in the great hall on the western bank of the Dead Sea drinking, smoking hashish, singing and playing music.

Because of its high concentration of salt it is almost impossible to swim in this sea, though no skill is needed to stay afloat in it. It has also been used to drown people's anger and as a repository for their curses and spells. One such invective was recently found by an archaeologist at the Hebrew University. In 2002 the sea had receded 200 metres from the beach and he was digging in the exposed land when he discovered two small packages of parchment wrapped in cloth. They were soaked in a preservative substance with a pungent odour resembling turpentine and folded in sheets of lead. When one of the packages was opened it was discovered to contain a scathing curse written in eloquent Arabic, most likely by a Palestinian from East Jerusalem after the Israeli invasion of 2002: 'O God Almighty, I beg you God to destroy Ariel Sharon, son of Devorah, son of Eve. Destroy all his supporters, loyal aides and confidants, and all those who love him and whom he loves among human beings and among devils and demons. Destroy them all, small and large, male and female, free men and slaves, kings and subjects, leaders and flock, soldiers who are all Satans. Destroy, O God, and annihilate Uzi Landau, the Minister of Public Security in the Israeli Zionist entity, son of Eve, and Tzachi Hanegbi, son of Geula Cohen, daughter of Eve, and also Shaul Mofaz, son of Eve, the Zionist chief of staff, Fuad Benjamin Ben-Eliezer, the captain of the host of the Israeli enemy, Moshe Katsav, Silvan Shalom, Moshe Ya'alon, Shin Beth head Avi Dichter, Yigal from intelligence in the East Jerusalem Minorities Unit, and James, who is in charge of the holy sites in Israeli intelligence. O God, destroy all their security and policing apparatus, their computers, their electronic and listening equipment.'

Four years later, on 4 January 2006, Ariel Sharon fell into a coma from which he has yet to recover. Perhaps the archaeologist was right to keep the second package unopened and the names of those who are cursed a secret. Perhaps it should be returned to the sea.

The sea shimmered so peacefully in the morning sun. I felt a strong desire to follow the great fault, travelling through the Rift Valley starting north in the Syrian plains, through Lake Qaraoun in Lebanon and down to the Dead Sea and Lake Tiberias, examining how it developed from geological pressures on the tectonic plates far below the surface of the earth. Regardless of Palestine and Israel, British colonialism and the geopolitical realities, I still want to travel through this valley, imagining it as it had once been, all one unit, undivided by present-day borders. But until the political problems of this region are resolved – a prospect unlikely in my lifetime – a trip like this will not be possible. For now, all I could manage after crossing four of the five checkpoints along my way to the Galilee was to take a moment to contemplate the view in my unceasing attempts to assert my freedom.

Leaving the Dead Sea, we made a left turn and began our trip on the road north, with the scanty waters of the river trickling down some distance to the right. Presently we came upon the secondary road that turns eastward to the Allenby Bridge, the main crossing point for Palestinians into Jordan. My heart began to beat faster as my fears were aroused by the sight of a long line of cars and buses halted along the road, waiting their turn to deposit passengers – hundreds of anxious, sweating Palestinians on their way to Jordan – made irritable by waiting in closed vehicles baking under the hot sun.

On a raised piece of ground on the hillside near the entrance to the bridge terminal, Israeli officials had used small stones to mark out the Star of David and nearby the insignia of the Israeli police, attempting to claim the land by adorning it with the symbols of their state. Like the seal stamped on our documents, this was just another way of indicating that the area was no longer considered occupied territory; it has been annexed de facto to Israel and placed under the jurisdiction of its Ports Authority. Driving from Ramallah, we had passed numerous other borders, borders within borders within borders. Everywhere I looked I could see borders, barbed wire and watch towers.

The best antidote to the claustrophobia we Palestinians feel while attempting to cross the many borders Israel has created is to focus our attention on the physical expanse of the land. Israel is attempting to define the terrain, to claim and fragment it with wire fences, signposts, gates and roadblocks staffed by armed soldiers backed up by tanks. I am but one of the millions of travellers who have passed through over the ages. I lifted my eyes and beheld the wonderful valley created eons ago as it stretches far and long, north to the Lebanon and south to the Red Sea and into Africa, utterly oblivious of the man-made borders that come and go.

As we drove further north along the river, I saw signs placed on the banks at frequent intervals saying, 'Border ahead – mined ground – do not enter or approach', reminding me that we're following what became Israel's new border after it occupied the West Bank of Jordan in the 1967 War. I was not convinced. The river is no more a border than the great fault. The only borders are in people's minds, artificial creations that come to be acknowledged and recognised by us, the people living here, because we have no choice. By creating this surfeit of borders, Israel has made a mockery of them and finally brought home the point that the only real borders are those which we come to accept. I hope I will never acknowledge that my tiny area of the West Bank has become separated into 227 geographical areas. I must always insist that I live in the region of Greater Syria along the Great Rift Valley.

For the first sixteen years of my life the River Jordan was not a border. The Hashemite Kingdom of Jordan extended along both sides of its banks. When we visited family in Amman, a mere ninety-minute drive from Ramallah, we felt only a slight tremor as the car drove over the wooden planks of the old rattle bridge. I always looked out of the window at the river rushing to the Dead Sea and felt sorry for the fish going to their death. I never saw anyone fishing, although it would have been kinder to catch the fish before they had to face the terrible ordeal of death by osmosis in water so high in concentrations of salt and other toxic substances that their insides would burst, a striking instance of the proximity here of sharp contrasts: fresh and salt water, life and death.

The Jordan has been called the river of the desert, highlighting another contrast. We call it Al Shari'a al Kubra (the great *shari'a*, or path to the headwater). This was also the name given to the Huleh, the swampy marshland north of Tiberias which Israel drained in the 1950s. In addition, *shari'a* (sharia) means faith, or the way. The Jordan is a fast-flowing river, one without a permanent course. It constantly twists and turns, luxuriating in the deep green valley through which it surges graciously and expansively. Not surprising, then, that it is the only river in the region with no major city on its banks.

The River Jordan is unique. Its waters cannot escape the valley in which it flows and nor can it be easily pumped. Before the river came to delineate a formidable border and access was prohibited, we only made fleeting visits to it. No cafes or rest houses were built along its banks. Once a year crowds would descend on it during the feast of the Epiphany to hear the Orthodox bishop conduct prayers. Then everyone would consume the food they had brought with them and leave. It wasn't a place to lay paths for walks along the banks because they are constantly shifting. It remains thus to this day. The river's contact with the history of the people has been exceptional, confined to rare occasions. This might explain why, unlike neighbouring Egypt with its Nile-fed land, Palestine continued over the ages to be sparsely populated and developed no great civilisation of its own.

In ancient agrarian economies agricultural production was always labour-intensive. Regions with the largest workforce possessed a vital natural advantage. Palestine could never compete with the riverine agrarian economic and demographic base of Egypt and neighbouring Mesopotamia. Nor, later, with Anatolia, Persia and eventually Europe in the form of the Greek and Roman powers that would come to dominate Palestine.

For a number of years the baptismal site on the River Jordan has been shifting ground. Israel conveniently located it along a slow-flowing tributary of the river just south of Lake Tiberias. There the faithful can come to be baptised without fear of being swept away by its swift current. A few years ago the Jordanian Ministry of Tourism proclaimed that archaeological and biblical evidence indicated that the site was in fact on Jordan's side of the river. Conveniently they located it close to the Dead Sea hotel area, with all its tourist amenities. What has become of the spirituality of the Apostle John, who said, 'God is spirit and those who worship Him must worship in spirit and truth'? Hilarion, one of the first monks, who came from Gaza and refused ever to visit Jerusalem, argued that 'God does not dwell in a particular place.' And still the faithful continue to approach the holy places with burning hearts and shining faces, rendering the Holy Land a profane battleground.

Sometimes the course of the river shifts in a single day. In the early years of the Israeli occupation of the West Bank, when security was still lax, a hunter from Jordan saw a purebred dog on the Israeli bank of the river. As he was preparing to leave in the afternoon, he saw that same dog standing on the Jordanian bank. The river had changed its course. He took the dog back home to Jordan and bragged to his friends that he had managed to smuggle out of the Occupied Territories a dog that did not carry an Israeli *tasreeh* (permit). For a long time afterwards it was claimed that the dog spent its days looking westward with an expression of yearning in its eyes.

The River Jordan once brought 1.3 billion cubic metres of water to the Dead Sea every year. It fed over 100 pumps drawing water to irrigate more than 10,000 *dunums* (a *dunum* is 1,000 square metres) of land that were cultivated on its western bank. It was still possible in 1847 to take a boat down the length of its course. A British naval officer, Thomas Howard Molyneux, sailed from Lake Tiberias to the Dead Sea, hoping to map the region. He was imprudent enough to make the journey in the heat of summer. Not surprisingly, it was an arduous expedition and when an exhausted Molyneux reached the Dead Sea he managed to take only a few measurements in the north before returning to his vessel in declining health. He died days later. The Dead Sea's southern extremity is named Cape Molyneux after him. The northern extremity is called Cape Costigan after an Irish predecessor who also succumbed at the end of his Dead Sea expedition in 1835. Cape Molyneux disappeared as the sea has receded and is now remembered only as a term in geography books.

Since the river's sources were diverted by Israel and, to a lesser extent, Jordan in recent times, the 1.3 billion cubic metres have dropped to less than 200 million. A large percentage of this diminished quantity is run-off from the agricultural communities and salt water diverted to the river from springs near the banks of Lake Tiberias. Some of the Jordan's water still comes from springs and streams that flow directly into the river. A few times in recent years the river has almost dried up altogether due to a shortage of rainfall.

I vividly recall my first encounter with a very different river. I was in the Swiss Alps in 1970, during my first trip outside the region. I was profoundly impressed by the raging river cascading down in waterfalls, splashing and roaring over rocks so much harder and darker in colour than our friable limestone. I had never encountered water sweeping down so persistently, so confidently, in such stark contrast to the hesitant waters of the Jordan. Water has always been a rare commodity, to be carefully used and saved. To see it rushing down so extravagantly and wildly was exciting and uplifting. I felt a sense of abandon and freedom. I was still in my late teens and it afforded me a sense of expansiveness, of unrestrained outpourings of energy and release, such as I had not felt since the Israeli occupation. I wrote poetry then and felt the verses gushing out of my head, creating a fountain of words that flowed as energetically and naturally as the river. I returned to Palestine with my poem and memories. When I read it back home I could hear the sounds and recapture the emotions the river had aroused in me. The minute I stopped I was back in the dry and miserable land of scarcity and restraint, a land struggling for resources, territory and water, a land under occupation mired in misery.

It was only in June 1967 that the River Jordan became a political border, more for symbolic value than military necessity. This was after the war between the Arab states and Israel broke out, causing hundreds of thousands of Palestinians – many of them already refugees from the Nakba of 1948 – to flee to Jordan, becoming twice refugees, like my uncle Fuad.

His flight happened in a most dramatic fashion. He lived in Ramallah and just after the bombs began to fall he was reminded of that day in April 1948 when he was twenty-three years old and was fired at by Jewish fighters. Then he had been travelling from his home in Jerusalem with his mother and a friend. They were heading for Ramallah in an attempt to escape the fighting. Just as they got to the turn at Nabi Yacoub, halfway to their destination, they came under a hail of bullets. The driver was killed and Fuad and his mother took shelter behind the car. But the shooting continued and he was hit in the back and his mother in the wrist. Both survived, but their ordeal remained with them. When the war started and he heard the shooting it all came back. The familiar world was blurred, mental maps were confused, towns and cities changed places. Ramallah became Jerusalem and, trying to escape, they lost their way. More than anything else they wanted to reach the river to cross over to safety. Along with some 100,000 Palestinians, my uncle and his family were going where Israel had long hoped that Palestinians would end up, leaving the West Bank vacant for Israeli Jews to settle it.

My father was adamantly opposed to leaving. 'I will die in my house rather than leave,' he had declared before the war. When he discovered that his brother had left, he immediately began making every effort to bring him back. Had my father chosen to leave in 1967 our family would have been spared the hardship of living for decades under Israeli occupation. I sometimes doubt whether our struggle will ever succeed in liberating us. What I've always been sure of is that, regardless of the cost, nothing proved more important in the fight against Israeli expansionist ambitions than our staying put on our land, our *summoud*.

During that historic June week the pressure of vehicles and people crossing to the east bank using the already bombed out Allenby Bridge was so heavy that the bridge collapsed and fell in to the river. Those fleeing had to walk across the crumbling remains that were half buried in the fast-running water. The crushed bridge symbolised the severing of ties between the two banks of the rogue river.

The war tore many families apart. Some were allowed back through a process of family reunification organised by the Red Cross. But many were denied the right. Among those was my classmate Abla, who was stranded in Jordan away from her family. After she realised her application for family reunification would never be accepted by the Israeli authorities, she and her brother hired a guide to lead them to where they could ford the capricious river. As soon as they had crossed they heard the sound of an Israeli army Jeep and had to hide behind bushes. As they crouched there they noticed the rotting corpses of other 'infiltrators' who had been shot earlier by the Israelis.

It took a number of years to internalise the new geography. The river where we used to celebrate the feast of the Epiphany and had had our picnics had become a lonely border river made inaccessible on either side by mines and barbed wire, a river that could only be glimpsed when there was a bend in the road as we drove along the heavily guarded border that it now marked.

Between Lake Tiberias and the Dead Sea, the Jordan covers a linear distance of about 100 kilometres but it winds through more than 200 kilometres to get there. During its course the river falls from 203 metres below sea level to 400 metres below at the Dead Sea. But I could not see any of this for myself as I sought to retrace Najib's footsteps. Only when the road climbed and curved eastward could I catch a glimpse of the fast-moving muddy river making its way south between bumpy mounds. Then the view would become exciting and I would crane my neck to see more before the car rounded another bend on its way north. All I could catch was a fleeting glimpse. Soon the river went out of sight, rushing unobserved down its eccentric path through the deep valley to the unavoidable encounter with the toxic waters of the Dead Sea.

How I would have liked to stop the car and walk down to the lonely river. But this would be too risky. The river has become a military border and if I were to be apprehended by an Israeli army patrol there would be no hope of convincing the soldiers that my purpose was not to guide infiltrators but to enjoy the river. With at least two lines of barbed wire and mined ground, I had to resort to memory and think of the pictures I have seen and the accounts of travellers going down the river. Among these was Mark Twain, who described the Jordan's course as 'so crooked that a man does not know which side of it he is on half the time'. The river is still crooked, but with the heavily guarded border and mined ground there can be no question these days as to which side one is on.

It is refreshing to think how, in the course of his flight from Ottoman soldiers, Najib was able to cross the river and reach the eastern bank without the need for visas or permits. He did so on horseback. It was not a serious matter. His horse plunged into the water at a place called Al Makhada (The Ford in the River). The water splashed about him and in no time Najib had reached the other side. He didn't need anyone's permission.

As we drove north I wondered how this area might have looked in Najib's day. Was the Jordan Valley arid this far south, with no cultivation and no human settlements? In an article he published in *Al Karmil* on 3 June 1925 he said he didn't believe the area was realising its potential. He had once described it as a miracle land, because it was not only one of the most fertile but also the lowest point on earth. The heat helped with the speedy growth of plants and trees and the early ripening of fruits, making it possible to sell the produce at a premium. Prior to the 1967 War, Jordan initiated a large-scale project to move water via channels from the River Yarmuk, which flows off the Golan Heights, to the north-east to the West Bank. This would have developed the agriculture in the region, but the project was abandoned after the occupation. Instead Israel proceeded to establish scores of farming settlements that depend on intensive irrigation. Forty million cubic litres per annum are pumped by Israel from the mountain aquifer for the use of its settlements in the area. This constitutes some 40 per cent of the annual renewable water in these basins. The Jewish population in these settlements is less than 5,000 but their consumption of water is equivalent to 75 per cent of the water consumption of the entire Palestinian population of the West Bank.

As I drove through the Palestinian communities of Zubeidat, Bardala and A'yn al Beida I thought of the land cases I have argued with Israeli officials who, on the pretext of security, have refused to allow these farmers access to land they own on the eastern side of the road. For the past forty-two years Israel has been preventing some 2,000 Palestinians who have left the Jordan Valley from returning to the area under the family reunification scheme, even for short visits, in an effort to keep them from again demanding their land back, citing security concerns. Thousands of *dunums* of Palestinian land have been illegally transferred to settlements and army bases in the area. The settlements that farm land seized from Palestinians employ Palestinians to work on the land. They also use cheap labour from Thailand. As I drove I could see a number of Asians riding their bicycles over the flat ground that is so ideal for cycling.

Those resilient Palestinian farmers who somehow managed to keep their land face discrimination in the allocation of water and have no easy access to markets to sell their crops. In 2006 the Israeli army enforced a policy of preventing Palestinian farmers from selling their produce to Israeli farmers at the nearest border crossing between the valley and Israel. Instead of travelling five kilometres, they were forced to travel fifty, to a distant cargo terminal at Jalameh and to wait endlessly at the internal checkpoints, causing their produce to spoil in the sun. Those who did not want to go that far were offering their produce for sale at roadside stalls, where their fresh produce gets polluted by the emissions of the speeding vehicles using the road.

None of these could be seen near land cultivated by settlers. But this is not the only way to distinguish lands farmed by Palestinians from those cultivated by the settlers. The enviable blue and red water mains indicating that the land is serviced by the Israeli water network are a giveaway. Then there is the more extensive use of greenhouses and mechanised farming, both of which are in most cases beyond the financial capacity of Palestinian farmers.

Virtually all of the land in the Jordan Valley, other than areas built up by the Palestinian population, has been placed under the jurisdiction of the settlement regional councils. This means that land not defined as belonging to a specific settlement is still off limits to Palestinians and in some instances is actively farmed by settlers. Almost all the settlements, despite tiny populations, leave huge footprints on the land, with extensive agricultural areas, large fields and greenhouses. Many now specialise in raising equatorial fish in an area where water is so precious.

The road we were driving north on, Route 90, is named Gandhi Road by the Israelis, in memory of Rehavam Ze'evi, the Minister of Tourism, who was assassinated by Palestinians. He was nicknamed Gandhi, not on account of his non-violent politics but because of his diminutive build. Ze'evi was the head of a political party in Israel that advocated 'transfer', a euphemism for the expulsion of Palestinians from their land. It must have seemed appropriate to those officials who gave the road this name because it would be the road Palestinians needed to cross on their flight east, as my uncle had done in 1967. More than anywhere else in the West Bank, the valley seems to be devoid of Palestinians. Palestinians living outside the Jordan Valley who own farmland here are separated from their property. Seven permanent checkpoints west of the Jordan Valley and north of the Dead Sea have been established and harsher restrictions are imposed by the army on Palestinians wanting to cross them. Unless they can prove that they live here they are not allowed to cross these barriers by car. Yet Israel makes it extremely difficult, if not impossible, to obtain building permits. And when Palestinians build homes without a permit, these are demolished by the army. In the village of Al 'Aqaba, which lies at the edge of the Jordan Valley and comprises 3,500 *dunums* of land, thirty-five of the forty-five structures of the village have received demolition orders because of 'lack of permit'.

After passing the first of these Gandhi Road signs I count five others. Vital road signs that drivers need are rarely in Arabic, but this one honouring Israel's Gandhi is; and just in case one misses it the first time it reappears again and again.

Another sign declares that the Jordan Valley is now called the Arvot Hayarden Regional Council. Israel long ago organised the West Bank into regional councils subject to Israeli laws and procedures. At one point near the road the army has dug a trench to prevent farmers from reaching their land. There are also military training zones where the Israeli army had been conducting exercises since the beginning of the occupation. The presence there of a firing zone helps destroy the traditional lifestyle of thousands of semi-nomadic or Bedouin shepherds in the area. They are frequently forced out of their tents and forbidden to graze their flocks in the area or to plant wheat and produce food.

The presence of these Bedouin encampments was vital to saving Najib's life. He was taken in by the Bedouins and concealed from the Ottoman soldiers who were looking for him. What worries the Israeli authorities is that in the middle of the last century a significant number of the Palestinian communities in the valley changed from seasonal extensions of villages in the northern West Bank into permanent communities. Only Israeli Jews are encouraged to settle in the valley, while every conceivable method is used to deter Palestinians from doing so. Not long ago the army demolished tents, tin huts and sheepfolds belonging to some twenty agricultural families in five places in the valley.

Driving further, we could see the remains of these demolished structures. These days destruction is caused by human intervention, but in the past it was natural disasters. The earth's crust between Jericho and Beisan is thinner than further north – two different crystal types are to be found adjacent to each other along the Rift Valley – and this has rendered the area susceptible to earthquakes that seem to occur at roughly 100-year intervals. The one in 1837 destroyed the town of Safed and the Arab villages in its vicinity. The earthquake of 1927 resulted in the partial destruction of Jericho, Beisan and Nablus, where 300 houses collapsed.

In 2004 and throughout 2007 and 2008 numerous tremors and minor earthquakes were recorded in the Jordan Valley, prompting seismologists to conclude that a major earthquake is heading this way. What is certain is that disaster for the region is looming, though whether brought about by human forces or by natural causes is yet to be seen.

It has been said that if the Galilee were paradise on earth, then the Jordan Valley city of Beisan would be its gate. But there is a new, far less idyllic gate further south, near the new border between Israel and Palestine, now marked by the wall being built by Israel on Palestinian territory. This new gate is a formidable sliding structure painted yellow, stretching the width of the road with barbed wire on each side. The main traffic crossing this border in both directions is made up of Israelis living on both sides. Most Palestinians are barred entry into 'the paradise' beyond.

As Penny and I stopped for inspection I watched the soldiers, young men and women, staffing this checkpoint. They wore strikingly tight clothes that emphasised their bodies. From behind their sunglasses, and in between messages exchanged over the mobile phones that seemed glued to their ears, they hurled instructions at the few Palestinians fortunate enough to be allowed through. These youngsters were convinced that the sophisticated surveillance material at their disposal, systems that their country has been developing, testing on the hapless Palestinians and exporting to various parts of the world, together with the free nature of the interaction among them, assured them recognition as part of the technologically developed, sexually liberated Western world. It also marked their separation from and superiority to the other inhabitants of the Arab Middle East in which they lived.

How markedly different the territory becomes once one crosses the checkpoint separating the West Bank from Israel. There are no more stalls or shacks, or any evidence of individual farms, because in Israel there are very few of those as sales are undertaken by a uniform marketing board rather than by individual farmers. There is also affluence, with greenhouses and sprinklers sending water arcing high up, creating rainbows as it sparkles in the sun before drizzling down on young seedlings. But the terrain is also different, because the Israeli area has a wider stretch of flat land before the western hills begin. This suggests that in 1948, when Israel was conquering the territory, it stopped at the point where the valley became narrower and less amenable to large-scale farming.

As we drove through I could see the lovely low hills by the side of the road and the higher Moab Mountains to the east of the river. I was gently wrapped in the folds of this huge fertile valley, with the fresh water of the beautiful Lake Tiberias further north and the productive land around the springs and small tributaries of the Jordan. Paradise indeed!

4

The Silence of the Land

Penny and I had left the central hills and the southern Jordan Valley and were driving north, where the southern tip of the Lebanon range slides without break into the plateau of Galilee. Here the hills are low and rounded, with smooth outlines and grass-covered uplands. No army camps to be seen anywhere. The dirty business of army practice had been moved soon after the 1967 War from Israel to the Occupied Territories.

At the eastern edge of this plateau on basalt rock stands the impressive Crusader fortress of Belvoir, which was built in the twelfth century by the Knights Hospitaller on 1.2 hectares of land. To reach it one has to ascend a couple of hundred metres on a narrow winding road. About two-thirds of the way up is a sign announcing the entrance to the Wadi Tavor Nature Reserve. At the top one is rewarded with the most gorgeous panoramic view. From sea level Belvoir stands at an altitude of just 312 metres, but the Jordan Valley, which it overlooks, is far below sea level and so lies 550 metres beneath the fortress. Life here must have been so good that the place came to be known as *coquet* (French for dandy).

Standing on the eastern side, where the terrain drops away sharply, one gets a perfect view of the Great Rift Valley, with the verdant Jordan Valley stretching as far south as the eye can see, a basin-shaped depression spread between the Moab Mountains, with their pink-rose colour, to the east and the plateau at the edge of which I stood. The fortress was so high and imposing that the Muslim forces under Salah al Din were unable to capture it after they defeated the Crusaders at Hittin in 1187. The capital city of Jerusalem was captured, as were the port city of Acre and the strong fort in Safad, before the Knights Hospitaller finally surrendered in 1189 after a siege that lasted one and a half years.

Until its occupation in May 1948 by the Golani Brigade, the Palestinian village of Kawkab al Hawa stood within the fortress walls, with extensions in a circle around it to the north and west. The village, which had been established in the eighteenth century, was wiped out in September 1948 after a kibbutz leader in the area asked the Israeli authorities for permission to destroy it along with three others in the vicinity. As I wandered beyond the barbed wire to the northern edge of the fortress, examining the few remains, I thought about its superb location and how fortunate its inhabitants must have been. A Muslim historian of the twelfth century described Belvoir as being 'built in a nest of eagles and the dwelling place of the moon'. Those who had once been blessed with living in this magnificent place and their descendants must now live in some overcrowded refugee camp somewhere in Lebanon. How could they have survived the loss of a village in such extraordinary surroundings? How were they ever able to describe it to their offspring who were born and grew up in the narrow lanes of an enclosed camp, never having seen it?

Like other Palestinian refugees, the inhabitants of this village still wait and expect to return to it. Between 1966 and 1968 Israel carried out excavations and reconstruction work in the fortress. Most traces of the Arab village were removed. Only a few ruins I was able to examine remain on the northern slope outside the fortress walls surrounded by barbed wire. Hundreds of thousands of tourists have visited the site without knowing that for some three centuries an Arab village thrived there, a much longer period than the Crusaders spent in the fortress. Israel established many new settlements in the Galilee on the land where Palestinian villages once stood. Not on these slopes. Only ghosts live here now.

I left the fortress and walked northwards. Wide vistas stretched before me in every direction. These Crusaders knew where to build their fortresses: always where they could survey the main routes. From here it would have been possible to see an army approaching from a great distance. Perhaps this is the only legacy they left behind, fortresses perched on strategic places throughout the Holy Land.

I was walking along a dilapidated road paved with stones and a few remaining slabs of tarmac left behind from the British Mandate, when secondary roads were built to link the various Arab villages together. The old road, now redundant, was in disrepair. I left it and walked on the new dirt road used by tractors, which were the only vehicles to drive here. Ahead was a wide expanse of green fields gently sloping downhill and there I began my descent. Tucked to the right and invisible to me was Wadi al Bira, the valley Najib rode through on his way to the eastern side of the river, where I intended to walk later. How different the land would appear to Najib were he to visit it now. The first thing to strike him would be the silence. I relished it as I stood surveying the scene. A gentle wind produced a soft susurrous sigh. But this was all. There was no other sound, not human, animal or machine. In Najib's time the hills would have been alive with the voices of other villagers and the noises of the farm animals – the cock, the donkey and the shepherd dog. There would be sheep and goats treading the trails, grazing. The muezzin's call to prayer would punctuate the day. All this has now gone. The cycle of nature has been broken, leaving nothing but green. No variety in colour or sound. No birds singing or bees buzzing about. The land has been swept clear of the life of the small farmer and the homesteads that had flourished for centuries. Breaking the prevailing silence is just the occasional swish of the clover as the wind sweeps down and blows through it.

I continued walking northwards, following the path along the dirt road surrounded on both sides by greenery that extended as far as the eye could see. I was descending from the edge of a beautiful, gently sloping, perfectly shaped bowl with nothing impeding my view in any direction. Living in the West Bank, I was not used to such open vistas of green cultivated fields so wide and lush. As I walked further the wind swept over my face from all sides, refreshing and energising. What a beautiful name had been given to this Arab village: Kawkab al Hawa, which is Arabic for star or planet of the wind. And how appropriate, because I felt I was on another planet.

Ahead of me, emerging from the great plain of Marj Ibn Amer and interrupting its continuity on the south-east, was Mount Tabor, a perfect breast-shaped hill where Christian tradition locates the transfiguration of Christ. The difference in topography between this area and the central hills helps explain the different patterns of land ownership. Because the land here is open and exposed, it was more difficult to secure. This meant that peasants needed the protection of strong local lords, who tended to be more intimately connected to the centres of power. Under the Ottoman system these lords collected taxes on behalf of the government. In the hilly parts of Palestine they were peasants themselves and there was a closer relationship between them and the other peasants. They cooperated, participated in the same social occasions and were often related by marriage. Not so in the Galilee, where the relationship was more feudal and distant. From around 1840 the peasants in the Galilee began cultivating not just for local consumption but also for export, whereas in the hills the main crops continued to be olives and grapes, neither of which were cash crops, as well as vegetables for local consumption. This meant that the peasants in the hilly areas could retain their independence. In the Galilee they planted cotton, sesame, barley and wheat, together with citrus in the coastal areas. Planting these crops for export meant that there were middlemen. This in turn involved complicated commercial transactions often necessitating loans. If the crops failed and they could not repay the loans they became embroiled in debts that further compromised their independence.

In 1858 the Ottomans enacted a land code, with regulations for land registration. Farmers in the hilly areas registered their land in their own names, whereas in the Marj they didn't. Here the farmers did not care about the formal ownership of the land. They inherited lands and exchanged them among each other as part of a cycle of crop rotation. They looked upon the feudal lord as their protector and did not mind if he registered the land in his name. Registration rendered land a commodity that could be bought and sold for the first time in the history of Palestine. Sometimes the buyers were not from the area. Among the outsiders was

Niqola Sursuq, one of the major merchants of Beirut, who in 1896, in cooperation with other Lebanese merchants Bustrus, Twaini and Farah, bought the lands of seventeen villages and towns in the Marj Ibn Amer plain. Between Nazareth, the Marj and the coast of Haifa, the Sursuq family owned 230,000 *dunums*, for which they paid just £20,000. In the early years of the twentieth century Sursuq hired thousands of workers to establish a modern cotton industry, only to suffer heavy losses. When the opportunity came to sell this land for a good price, some of these feudal lords sold large tracts to the early Zionists. There were others from Palestine and absentee landlords from elsewhere who sold land to the Zionists, but the name of Sursuq remains associated in the mind of many Palestinians with what they deem to be the greatest of villainy: selling land to the enemy. In the mythology I'd forgotten that the Ottoman land law reform had rendered land a resource that could be bought and sold and Sursuq was merely a businessman who needed cash for his extensive investments. But even with willing vendors such as these Lebanese landlords, by the time the Jewish state was established the Zionists had succeeded in acquiring only 6.8 per cent of the land. The rest was acquired by conquest.

In the area where I was walking the settled Bedouin tribes of Al Ghazzawiyya, Al Bashatiwa and Al Saqor constituted the greatest part of the valley's population and were of vital help to Najib over ninety years ago. They provided him with shelter and fed him the dairy products for which they were famous. The villagers lived in both permanent dwellings and tents. They tended their animals in the Jordan Valley in winter and in the highlands in summer. In 1948 all three tribes were forced out to the eastern side of the Jordan.

Encircling Mount Tabor are the villages of Dabburiya to the west, Um al Ghanam (mother of goats) south of the hill and Arab al Shibli to the north-east. Only their names now betray the origins of these last two villages as belonging to herdsmen and goat farmers. No longer do their inhabitants have any goats to graze or land to farm. Most of their land has gone. Like most Arab villages in Israel, they look cramped and unhappy. And rather than hug, they choke the hill. Close to the south I could see the Arab villages of Tamra, Na'ura and, further south, Taybeh t'al Zoubi. I had brought along a small notebook in which I had recorded the names of the villages and Bedouin encampments where Najib had stopped and was given food and protection. I checked whether the names of any of these villages were mentioned in my notes. None were. Where, then, could Najib have hidden? Where were the villages that had sheltered him? Closer to me was the Jewish village of Moledet (Hebrew for homeland). It was greener, with an abundance of trees and gardens. It looked more relaxed and less crowded than the Arab villages. It also had gates that were closed on Saturdays. The road from the main Beisan–Tiberias highway that went west did not reach the Arab village. How well I knew from my West Bank experience the politics of road construction.

Mount Tabor dominates the horizon, rising above the plains, imposing because it is the only significant bluff in an otherwise flat terrain. Yet it makes no attempt at impressing, as mountains often appear to be doing; it is but a gentle benevolent presence well situated, well rested on the ground, almost globular, unmoving yet a commanding enough presence to remind us that it sits there much more firmly rooted in the landscape than any of us transient beings. It has been there for centuries, from the time of the Canaanites and Hebrews, Greeks and Romans, Muslims and Crusaders, Ottomans and the Europeans who drove them out, and it will be there long after all of us are gone. It was called mountain by those who wanted to give it the respectability and stature of a mountain which it does not need. We are told that from the dawn of history it was a place where humanity found contact with the unknown.

As we walked Penny said, 'I find the whole terrain strange.'

'How?' I asked.

'Like a fairy-tale land.'

'To me it feels more like a ghost land.'

It was as though everything on these hills had been cleared away, leaving uninterrupted swathes of slightly inclined plains that were now cultivated with clover and wheat. Yet despite forcing out most of the Arabs in 1948 and despite the discriminatory practices of successive Israeli governments, those who managed to stay now constituted the bulk of the population in the Galilee. Their numbers are not proportionate to the area of land they own. The Jewish minority controls most of the land, just as in the Jordan Valley further south in the Occupied West Bank.

Depending on what one is doing, the land looks different. To Najib when he was hiding it must have seemed so exposed, with nowhere to hide. He must have dreaded the greater visibility that I was enjoying so much.

We had walked for two hours now and since leaving the ruins of Kawkab al Hawa had not spotted the remains of any other Palestinian village. Where were those villages in which Najib hid from the Ottoman authorities? I began to suspect that perhaps we had come to the wrong place.

Taking large stretches of land and developing water schemes to serve them were part of the grand plan conceived by the Zionist colonialists from the early part of the last century. The extent of arable land in the Galilee and abundance of water encouraged such grandiose plans. The Zionists were able to find some willing vendors. But it was in 1948 that they had the opportunity to clear large areas of the land of the Palestinian villagers who inhabited it. They acquired more land than they could have dreamed would ever be theirs. Those Palestinians who managed to remain on their land were confined to small areas and most of the land they had cultivated was taken away from them. The dream of the early Zionists was realised more successfully than they could ever have expected. The empty stretches of land spread before me were proof of their success.

As I walked further downhill I wondered why the inhabitants of some Arab villages had been allowed to remain while others had been forcibly evicted, especially since the evacuation in most cases was not connected to the war effort and had taken place in 1949, a year after the establishment of the Israeli state.

Looking at the deserted slopes, I could only think that some Zionist commanders must have been concerned with creating vast expanses of cultivable land that would make mechanised farming easier and saw the Arab villages as standing in their way. It reminded me of the Highland Clearances, the forced expulsion of the Gaelic population of the Scottish Highlands in the eighteenth and nineteenth centuries in order to turn their land into grazing ground for sheep.

When we finally reached the bottom of the slope and began walking to Taybeh we heard the muezzin's call to prayer breaking the deep silence. At the outskirts of the village were grasslands but no cultivated fields, probably because the land had been confiscated. The village we approached smelled and looked like a farming village, only it had no farms. The poppies in the surrounding grassland were in bloom. I stopped to rest and saw the caterpillar nests in the green weeds, like webs of dew swarming with curled-up tiny creepers. I could smell the intoxicating odour of fresh grass. The rocks jutting out of the grass were dark-coloured like steel, black and brown with yellow mustard seed bunched up around them. Here and there the green was highlighted with the deep blue lupins that grow only in these hills.

Taybeh was not a typical village because, unlike Dabburiya, it was not choking. It felt more relaxed and spread out, with homes that were not piled on top of one another. Perhaps this was because the Zoubi clan, who controlled the place and gave it its name, had good relations with the Israeli establishment and were able to negotiate for more land allocation. Or perhaps these were illegally built houses which were saved from demolition by the Israeli authorities through the good offices of the local council of the village. These were the same tactics I was familiar with in the West Bank, discriminatory town planning that for the Arab areas is designed to isolate, stifle and restrict development.

In an Arab village I once visited in the Galilee I saw one of the most cynical consequences of such policies. Samih, the young son of the family, had a degree in criminology and after years of unsuccessful attempts to find work he accepted a job with the Israeli police. He was appointed to a station in Occupied East Jerusalem, where he participated in the interrogation of Palestinians from the Occupied Territories. He was living in a rented flat in the Jewish settlement of Maaleh Adumim. Despite his almost total embrace of the Israeli system, he could not fulfil his most cherished dream of building a house with a garden for his family in his village. The family owned land close to the village but outside the Israeli town-planning scheme. Much as he tried to convince the Israeli authorities to grant him a building permit, even going to the extent of writing to the president of the state, he was unable to obtain one. He was told by the planning authority that they did not want any building in locations designated as 'green areas'. Across from his land, in the same green area, he could see a new Jewish village being constructed which had been issued with permits by the same authority that had denied him his. Being in law enforcement, he could not – as many of his fellow villagers were doing – just flout the law and build on the land he owned without bothering with a permit. They might have reconciled themselves to paying a yearly penalty, but it would have been beyond his means to pay, even if he had wanted to break the law. So, from the cramped rooms in his father's home, Samih looked longingly at the plot standing vacant with a few olive trees that he could not turn into his cherished home and garden.

After our walk I saw Samih working in the garden. I expressed regret that he was not growing any herbs. My remark seemed to strike him as a criticism. Using the technique he must have learned in his training with the Israeli police, he tried to neutralise my assumed aggression. In a deep, patronising voice calculated to sound friendly he began with a greeting: 'First of all, a good morning to you, sir.' It was a way of speaking that reminded me of how Israeli officials in the military government spoke to Arab heads of village councils. Yet all I was doing was suggesting that he grow parsley!

By the time we got to Taybeh we were parched. We had drunk all the water we had brought with us and needed to top up. It had been tiring walking in the hot sun. We stopped a young boy to ask for a shop where we could buy drinks. He was blond and fair-skinned, with green eyes.

'You are a Zoubi?'

Not far from here was the village of Kufr Cana, where Najib was stopped by Ottoman soldiers. It was the fair features of a Zoubi that had saved him from being captured. He was still hiding in Nazareth when the army came looking for him. So he had tried to get to Kufr Cana, a small village with a famous spring by the slope of the hill at the outskirts of Nazareth. He had left the city intending to stay with his friend Abu Naif, the *mukhtar* (mayor) of the village. He never made it. Just after passing the spring where he planned to stop, he saw mounted soldiers near the house. He turned his horse round and began to head back to the main road, but one of them saw him, left the others, raced ahead and waited for him at the crossroads. Najib saw the man standing with his rifle pointed at him. He had to decide in an instant whether to use the gun he was carrying, shoot between the legs of the horse and take off as fast as he could, or risk stopping. He decided to stop.

Najib must have been easy to identify. He had a fair complexion and large brown eyes. He sat on his horse straight-backed and broad-shouldered. With his fair features he could pass for a German. His only disguise was his outfit: he was not dressed like a Haifa gentleman but wore a long shirt over which he had wrapped a camel-skin cloak. His head was covered with a white keffiyeh and an *aqal* (black coiled rope to keep the headdress in place).

'*Es salaamu aleikum,*' Najib greeted the soldier in his strong, imperious voice.

The soldier returned the greeting, then asked, 'Where to?'
'Tiberias.'

As he was replying, Najib noticed that the man had fair skin. 'You must be from the Zoubi family, are you not?' he asked, before the soldier could hurl more questions at him.

'If my mother told me the truth, yes,' answered the soldier.
'Then how is Ali Muhammad Said,' asked Najib.
'Which one?'
'Both, Muhammad Said al Abeed and Muhammad Said es Soumali.'

'Both are well.'

'God be praised. Would you be so kind as to pass my greetings to them?'

'Whom should I say is sending them?'

'Tell them a friend from Ijzim.'

With this the soldier turned his horse and returned to Kufr Cana. He was too embarrassed to investigate someone who appeared to be a friend of the family.

As I sipped my drink at the shop, I checked the old map again and saw that at least ten Arab villages had stood on the side of that slope I had just descended but no trace of any of them could be seen. I remembered reading that a number of villages in this area had mixed Muslim, Christian and Jewish populations. All the villages in the Galilee are now segregated along Arab and Jewish lines.

Our original plan had been to walk back through Wadi al Bira, following the route Najib had taken on his way to the eastern bank of the Jordan. We saw a young man in shorts sunning himself in his garden while listening to a Hebrew broadcast. We asked him for directions to Wadi al Bira. 'I don't know,' he answered. Then he said, 'Perhaps you mean Wadi Tavor. It is over there to the right. Continue straight up this road, make a right and you will see it.'

I checked the Israeli map and the area where Najib had walked, Wadi al Bira, had indeed been renamed Wadi Tavor. It had also been turned into a nature reserve with marked walking trails. I remembered that we had seen its southern entrance as we drove up to Belvoir. If we were to go back through the wadi we would have to walk up the road to the top of the hill where we had parked the car.

The sun was high in the sky and we were tired, yet we had still not come across the remains of a single village or encampment through which Najib had passed.

*

A short distance west of the old road in a field I could see a tree in bloom. It turned out to be an almond. Now, an almond is not the kind of tree that grows on its own. It is always cultivated. But why would the people who worked these fields plant an almond tree in the middle of nowhere? Then I noticed scattered rocks. They stood out in the field. I could not make out whether they were the remains of a wall or the borders of graves. Still, it was clear that these were the ruins of one of the many Palestinian villages that had once stood here. But which? There was no sign or plaque to commemorate it.

I looked for other trees and began to see more of them emerging from the sea of green. Their dark trunks were submerged in the undergrowth and all I could see were black branches covered with white blossoms shooting into the air to form a radiant bush.

Almond blossoms are a celebratory white, adorned with a single pink spot at the base where the petals and stamens join. They cover the tree like satin sleeves, making the branches that shoot into the air seem so light and airy. Each year, ever since the farmers who lived in the villages were forced out, these almond trees have been blossoming, their glorious white flowers marking the approaching end of winter and the coming of spring.

The wind blew, lifting up some of the petals, which then flew into the air. They clouded the area where the village had once stood with a white mist before gently falling over the green wheat like snowflakes on a bright spring day, flimsy white dots on the green. When, later in the year, the blossoms turn into the green velvety fruit there will be no one to pick them and taste the intense flavour of springtime in their crunchy flesh. They will remain on the tree until they harden and their skin turns into a black leathery sheath that will eventually fall to the ground, to be picked up and crushed by the heavy mechanical plough.

With the almond trees as my markers, I began to survey the fields again and reconstruct in my mind what the villages had looked like and how Najib must have galloped from one to the other as he escaped capture by the Ottoman soldiers. Many more trees must have been felled, just as human beings have been cleared, to leave open fields where machines could work unhindered at sowing and harvesting the wheat. The few trees that were left to provide coordinates for the men working the machines were the only reminders of the life that had once flourished here, peaceful presences above the grassy land, marking where the houses, schools, mosques, churches and cemeteries of the old villages had been, singular reminders of an Arab presence that had long since been uprooted out of existence.

When I looked at the open green fields spread on both sides of my path I could see more almond trees that I had failed to notice before I recognised their significance. They now provided me with a matrix of the possible locations of the destroyed villages. There to the west Kufra must have stood and nearby to the south Bira, Dana and Tireh. With the possible location of the Arab villages, the old features of this cemetery of a land began to emerge, illuminated by the white blossoms of the almond trees, marked by the petals that slowly glided down to the ground around them in utter, hushed silence.

5

One of the Last Survivors of Ottoman Times

Ever since I had heard from Basel, the young picnicker by the carob tree, about his great-great-grandfather, one of the few contemporaries of Najib still alive, I had wanted to visit the old man. But it was only in 2007, after the Second Intifada that I was able to travel up to the Galilee to meet Abu Naif in Kufr Cana, the village where Jesus is said to have turned water into wine.

Najib's account of his time as a renegade during the Great War provides a strong sense of relations during that period between Arabs and Turks but not of the problems ordinary people had to endure during those horrendously difficult years. What he chose to write about and what he chose to omit tells much about his character. He is a romantic who wants his readers to appreciate the pleasures of the simple life of the peasant and Bedouin, so he does not dwell on the inconveniences and difficulties. He is also pursuing a political agenda. By pointing out the positive aspects of life under the Ottomans, he is distinguishing it from how things had become under the British Mandate, with its discriminatory policies against the Arabs in favour of the Jews.

Although his account is described as a novel, it provides the reader with no sense of the atmosphere of turbulent times marred by famine and pestilence. Instead he is always being offered great hospitality by his Bedouin hosts, many of whom insist on slaughtering a sheep to feed him. Nor does he mention anything about the devastation of the countryside brought about by the attack of locusts in 1915 that destroyed agriculture in the Galilee. And of the typhus epidemic that killed so many people, he says only that it also did away with the life of the German consul who caused him so much trouble by trying to recruit him for the Axis powers. It was in the hope of getting a better sense of the times that I travelled up to the Galilee again to visit Basel's aged relative and continue my walks along the trail that Najib had followed.

Basel invited me to the house where he lived with his wife and young child for refreshments. We climbed the stairs to the second floor and entered the combined living and dining room, which boasted a truly fascinating display of showy furniture lining the walls. The young couple must be enamoured of glitter, I thought. Every article of decor was a different colour. The centrepiece was a replica of the Dome of the Rock in mother-of-pearl. I sat on a huge armchair upholstered in crimson velvet. It could have accommodated three men of my size. Basel wanted me to linger in his house to give his great-great-grandfather time to get back home.

'He went out?' I asked, surprised. 'Where did he go?'

'To the mosque. He goes every day. And all alone. He refuses to let anyone help him.'

After drinking lemonade and eating some delicious oriental sweets, we made our way to the old man's home.

Abu Naif lived in a ground-floor flat with a patio at the front. When we got there he had still not returned. I looked around. No ostentation here: simple furniture, a bed on one side, some old chairs with wicker seats and a shelf stacked with papers. I went over to have a look. Basel picked up a folder and took out a clipping from a yellowed West Bank newspaper that had interviewed his great-great-grandfather a few years ago.

As I was reading, Abu Naif entered. He was a tall, thin man, slightly bent, carrying a cane and wearing a djellaba with an *abba* over it, perhaps the same type of clothing he had worn during Ottoman times. He shook my hand in greeting with a firm grip even though his skin was soft like cigarette paper. He scrutinised me with clear eyes from behind glasses and welcomed me. He spoke a few words to Basel. It was apparent that the two enjoyed a close and loving relationship. I noticed how respectful and solicitous the young man was towards his great-great-grandfather. He seemed to hover about him, trying to be unobtrusive, for the old man obviously did not want to be fussed over and guarded his independence. I could see that Basel would be very sad when the old man finally died. After being around for so long, he would leave a huge void in the lives of his numerous descendants.

Abu Naif stood his cane behind the door and went to sit on the floor on a thin mat that had been placed between the bed and the door. I knew this would be a long session and I've never learned to be comfortable sitting on the floor. I thought of sitting on the bed but decided instead to drop to the floor next to the old man, leaning my back against the bedstead.

'You need a cushion behind your back,' Abu Naif said.

'No. I'm all right. This is enough.'

'Basel,' the old man called, 'bring a cushion.'

He did and handed it to me. I thanked him and placed it behind my back sideways.

'No,' said Abu Naif. 'Not this way, the other way.'

I began to protest that this was comfortable enough the way it was when Basel looked at me and said, 'Do what he asks or he will keep after you until you do.'

It was good advice and we finished talking of the cushion and how I should arrange my limbs. Having lived all these years, the old man has surely earned the privilege of being obeyed, I thought.

In one of the land cases I had handled we had needed a sworn statement from a man who, like Abu Naif, had lived in Ottoman times. After writing the man's name, I asked him for his place of birth, which he readily gave. But when I asked him for his date of birth, he adamantly refused to divulge it.

'Why?' I had asked.

'You don't know why?' he asked warily, looking around to see if anyone was eavesdropping. 'What if the authorities should find out?'

'Find out what?' I asked.

'My age.'

'Why should they care?'

'You don't know why?' he questioned, his voice betraying suspicion.

I admitted I didn't.

The old man looked at me as though I was in league with those who were trying to get him.

Now I asked, 'Which authorities?'

He didn't answer, but said, 'You want them to know I lied about my age?'

He was still concerned that the Ottoman police would know he had lied about his age to escape conscription in the First World War.

From what I could tell, Abu Naif had no such apprehensions. He had a clearer understanding of the times and seemed to be living more fully in the present. I began by asking him what he remembered of Ottoman times. He cleared his voice, invoked Allah and his prophet Muhammad and began to speak.

'*Hukm al Attrak* [the Turks' rule] was terrible. They were cruel, hungry beggars. They built no schools or mosques. They destroyed the country and left nothing green in it. They were like the locusts that swept over the country in the spring of 1915, destroying everything green. Every six days we were all supposed to fill a sack provided by the government with dead insects. When we presented it to the *hakim* [governor] we were given a certificate. Anyone found without a current one had to pay a penalty of one riyal [Ottoman currency]. The Turks robbed us of everything and gave us nothing back. Those were terrible times. Four hundred dark years. Their army was an army of thieves and beggars. We used to hide the wheat so they wouldn't steal it. They would raid the village periodically, looking for food and firewood. They cut down so many of the trees around the town. All the hills were forested. By the end of the war very few trees were left. Yes, *ya Basha* [Pasha, a form of address common during Ottoman times], those were difficult times. My father was killed when I was still in my mother's womb. The Turks hanged him. I never knew him. I was an only child. My grandfather took care of me. He was a tough man. Very hard. I was his only grandson. He was determined that I should survive. He raised me and took care of me. He was 106 when he died. God rest his soul and preserve it.'

Clearly, longevity ran in Abu Naif's family.

Abu Naif turned to look at Basel, wishing him and me long life, adding, 'with good eyesight and memory, *insha'allah*'.

I was going to comment that I would be satisfied with a few years less than 106, but he began to speak again.

'I have one hundred grandchildren,' he announced proudly.

His grandfather would have been proud of him. Surely he has made up for the premature death of his own father, who left only one descendant, I thought.

'When the war ended I was fourteen. But I was tall. I looked older than my age. My grandfather was worried that I would be taken on *safar barlik*. Those who went never returned.'

I could hear the fear in his voice as he uttered the dreaded Turkish words *safar barlik*, which at the time must have evoked certain death. Everyone knew that going to the front would be the last journey, from which there would be no return, the final farewell.

'There was a secret tunnel in the village underneath the centre. Whenever soldiers were sighted approaching, I would be taken down there to hide.'

I asked whether it was still possible to visit the tunnel.

'Not any more. The Jews have closed it.'

I wondered whether Najib would have known of this tunnel and whether he had ever considered hiding there.

'One day the army came to the village and stayed for a long time. They would not leave. As long as they were there I could not come out. I remained in the dark tunnel with its black mouldy walls for days.

'My grandfather had the idea of finding me a foreign woman to get married to, because men who were married to foreign women were not conscripted.'

'Why is that?'

He looked at me as though I were a halfwit.

'Because then, after the man goes away, the woman would be left by herself in a village to which she does not belong. This would be dangerous. It could lead to immoral behaviour.

That's why villages made deals with distant villages. You give us ten women and we'll give you ten in exchange. This was how each village would save ten more men from the dreaded *safar barlik*. The fortunate men were those who came from Jerusalem. In those days people were referred to by the name of their place of origin. So if you were Ahmad al Makdisi [Ahmad of Jerusalem] the Turkish soldiers took good care of you. They did not put you on the front line. They made sure you were always surrounded by other men so you did not get shot and die. Jerusalem is a holy city. Anyone from there must have been touched by holiness, they believed. They had great respect for anyone from Al Quds.'

He recited two lines of poetry about the knights of Jerusalem, hesitating slightly at the second verse before the words came. When he finished he looked at me expectantly, perhaps awaiting applause.

'Why aren't you taking notes?' he asked.

'I can remember everything,' I said.

'Take notes,' he ordered.

Basel cast me the same look he had used when I resisted positioning the cushion in the manner favoured by Abu Naif. I obediently took out my small black notebook and asked him to repeat the lines, dutifully writing them down this time. He looked pleased.

Throughout my visit the old man remained seated on the floor, his back resting against the bare wall, knees bent close to his chest, while I sat with my cushioned back against the bedstead, legs stretched before me. Soon one of my legs went numb. I shifted. Abu Naif never stirred. He remained in the same place, keeping the same position, for the entire hour and a half that he spoke. Every once in a while he would tuck his *abba* under his thigh, smoothing it with his delicate bony hands. He was a proud, dignified old man, and when he forgot a name he would not go on until it came back to him. It must be good for one's memory to have a hundred offspring. The mere effort of remembering all their names would be exercise enough for the mind. Abu Naif's only visible frailty was that he was hard of hearing. This was the only sense that seemed to have failed him. I had to sit close to him and speak as loudly as I could into his left ear. Our heads were so close together that when he spoke I could smell his breath. I was impressed at how sweet it was. He must have good gums, I thought.

I asked him whether he had ever smoked.

'Only for two months. Then someone told me it was bad for the health. I took the tobacco which we grew and my pipe, the whole lot, and traded them for the labour of a man ploughing two *faddans* of my land.'

I asked him whether he knew Turkish.

'Only the *bashawat* [plural of pasha] who worked for the government could speak it. Otherwise everyone spoke Arabic.'

I asked him whether he knew a man by the name of Najib Nassar.

'Who is he?' he asked.

'A journalist from Haifa.'

Abu Naif looked at me as though I were a lunatic. Immediately I realised what a silly question I had asked. Here was a farmer whose education ended at second grade, as he had proudly announced. He spent much of the war years hiding in a tunnel. He considered the women who came from the next village as foreigners. He probably never saw a newspaper throughout his youth, let alone read one. He might never have visited Haifa as a young man and yet I wanted him to know my great-great-uncle, a foreigner, a man of letters and in his eyes a pasha!

Abu Naif looked at his grandson and announced, 'This

man doesn't know how to ask questions. Why is he quizzing me about the rulers?'

'What would you like me to ask you?'

'Ask me about the rebellion against the British.'

'Tell me.'

Relieved, Abu Naif tucked his *abba* under his thigh once more and proceeded to speak in great detail about his involvement in the 1936 uprising against the British and Zionist forces, how he was arrested, put on trial and sentenced to death by hanging, and how at the last minute his sentence was commuted to long-term imprisonment.

Abu Naif was only fourteen when Ottoman rule ended, too young to have formed a distinct sense of personal identity beyond family and village. His national identity developed at the time of heightened Palestinian nationalism during the British Mandate. This was unlike Najib, who thought of himself as an Ottoman citizen, as he proudly declares in his writings. He saw no contradiction between being a Christian and an Ottoman, because the empire was multi-ethnic, the kind of political entity we have come to long for today.

Wishing to take a break from the distant past, I asked Abu Naif what he thought of Israeli rule. I wanted to know how he, born in an empire that had ruled here for 400 years and as one who had witnessed its shameful defeat and the retreat of its army, once great then hungry, sick and beggarly, would think of the 1948 war and the ignominy that followed it. But much as I tried to steer him away from his glorious years in the 1936 Great Arab Revolt, he refused to comment on present times. Perhaps experience had taught him to be careful in what he says about the authority in power. Or perhaps his numerous offspring had warned him, for their own safety and his, against being loose-tongued. At least he was not like my affidavit man – one of my clients – still believing the Ottomans were in power and about to trick him into exposing his little deception.

What I heard from Abu Naif about the war years confirmed what I had learned from my grandmother Mary Sarrouf, the second wife of Boulos, my paternal grandfather, whose family, like all the inhabitants of Jaffa, was forced to evacuate the city soon after the Ottomans joined the war. The same fate befell the inhabitants of Gaza City. Her father escaped conscription by hiding in the Nablus hills. She and her five sisters went with their mother to Damascus, where they had acquaintances. To survive they had to bake pastries to sell in the street. A year later they travelled by train to join their father in Nablus. There they suffered two years of hunger and destitution. She would tell us how people were so hungry they went after the dung dropped by the horses of the Ottoman soldiers, dried it and picked out the undigested grain, then cooked and ate it. They searched through the garbage for potato peelings. They searched the hills around town for edible herbs and, if they found any, felt as happy as if they had unearthed buried treasure. Although she lived well into her nineties and, through the work of her son, became affluent, she never wasted any food or piece of cloth, however small. When her son stopped wearing a fez she turned its felt into crimson slippers. Those difficult years of famine and pestilence marked her for the rest of her long life.

Boulos's first wife and the natural mother of my father, Aziz, was less fortunate. Boulos travelled to Jenin to help his brother the medical doctor and to escape conscription, and his wife accompanied him. Soon after they got there she contracted typhus, which was known to be contagious. Her young son, who was three at the time, was taken away and not allowed to be anywhere near his dying mother. She had a continuous cough, a rash over her entire body, a high fever, a faint heartbeat and was delirious and confused. The child yearned for a last hug from her, but she died before she could give him one. To the end of his life my father suffered not only from having lost his mother at a young age but from not being allowed to kiss her goodbye.

The final years of Ottoman rule were a time of fear of conscription, of famine and disease. They overshadowed everything that had preceded them, so not surprisingly this is what stood out in the minds of those who survived them and these are the memories that were passed on to subsequent generations. With those miserable four last years of the war coming to represent over four centuries of Ottoman rule, everyone agreed that *hukm al Attrak* constituted this region's darkest age, when the country was robbed of its resources and its able young men, while the people were kept sick, hungry, impoverished and illiterate.

The facts, however, were otherwise. The Ottomans established schools and hospitals. The *Tanzimat* (literally 'reorganisation') period in the nineteenth century brought about impressive administrative reforms. This was also the time when extensive improvements were carried out to the legal system, promulgating codes on many different subjects. Of these the land and civil codes survived until recently in a number of countries in the Middle East. They continue to be in force in the Palestinian Territories. The Ottomans instituted the *millet* system, which allowed each religious community a measure of independence. The beautiful wall around the Old City of Jerusalem which still stands was built by them. Many attractive water fountains were erected all over the city, as well as orphanages like the monumental Khaski Sultan building in Jerusalem. They constructed roads between main urban centres and railway lines that connected the far-flung parts of the empire. But perhaps their most important legacy was uniting the region and relieving it for four centuries from the horrors of exterior invasions that had devastated it for many years before. In the Ramallah area, one of the best schools, Al Hashemieh, which survives to this day, was established by the Ottomans. They also built the attractive old building near the school I attended that served as the police station until 2002, when it was destroyed by Israeli fighter planes. Ottoman rule left a richer legacy than those desperate final years of the empire suggest and Najib's writings offer a nuanced view. Since then, revisionist historians have presented a more balanced assessment of the Ottoman period, but Najib was one of the earliest writers to take that line. And, even more surprisingly, he was one of the rare few to lament the empire's demise.

So much happened to Najib during the Great War. His wife deserted him and he became estranged from his children. He had to live in penury and depend entirely on the kindness of strangers, and yet those were years when, along with the worst, he also experienced the best of the human spirit: generosity, courage and solidarity. There were those who betrayed him and told lies about him to the authorities. In most cases these were fellow Christians from the cities, while those who took great risks to help him escape hanging, after he left Nazareth, were Muslim villagers and Bedouins.

The experience of living in the countryside in villages and Bedouin encampments brought Najib closer to ordinary people, farmers, peasants and Bedouins, whom he came to respect greatly. In later years it saddened him to see the life of many of these groups destroyed by the allure of cash, which began to be more available than ever in Palestine. The end of the war and the dismantling of the Ottoman Empire marked the termination of Najib's world. This was not only because he had been comfortable in his identity as an Ottoman, but also because, long before others, he was concerned about the effect that the new wave of nationalism sweeping the empire would have on the future of Palestine. As a multi-ethnic structure, the Ottoman system incorporated widely diverse people, adherents of all three monotheistic Abrahamic religions. Economically the empire might have been doing poorly, especially in its last years, but it was not colonialist and had no plans to deprive people of their land or exploit their resources. People used their own language; there was no imposition of the Turkish language or culture. And after the constitution of 1876 was enforced, there was a substantial measure of freedom of expression that allowed Najib and others to establish newspapers, publish books and make public speeches. Before the war various reformist ideas had been floating around for developing and modernising the Ottoman system. In most cases the objective was change rather than a total dismantling of the system.

On 5 February 1877 the spirit of hope was at its peak. The high-flown rhetoric reflected it. Except for the fact that the Ottoman parliament, which convened in Istanbul, did not include women, it has been considered by some as the greatest democratic experiment in history. It was the first time that representatives of different religious communities and races from three continents, Asia, Africa and Europe, speaking fourteen different languages, met together. As was required by law, they all knew some Turkish and spoke something called 'rough Turkish', which was different from the Ottoman language used by the educated elite of Istanbul and was a pastiche of Turkish, Arabic and Persian, with the last two constituting some 50 per cent of the words. 'Rough Turkish' was the language of the common people. It contained short, simple sentences and proved an adequate means of communication in assembly deliberations. One representative declared,

'Serving the entire society is the intention of parliament. When this is the case, there is no need to differentiate by religion.' Another proclaimed, 'Discrimination is against the constitution. Let no such discussion occur here. Let us refrain from terms such as "Muslim" and "non-Muslim", Greek and Armenian. Let us not speak such words here again.' Manok Efendi of Aleppo argued, 'We are not becoming Ottomans now; we have been Ottomans for four hundred years. Thanks to our Sultan, our Ottomanism has been strengthened.'

The constitution that gave birth to the parliament was part of the process of modernisation that had begun during the first half of the eighteenth century. Although short-lived, the parliamentary intentions of the constitution reflected the practical aim of saving a decaying empire from collapse by creating one Ottoman nation out of many Ottoman subjects. The assembly held two sessions, the first from March to 28 June 1877 and the second from 13 December 1877 to 16 February 1878. In April 1877 Russia declared war against the Ottoman Empire. An allowance for 600,000 soldiers had been authorised by parliament, but only half that number had apparently been engaged in battle. Although not stating this openly, the deputies believed that Sultan Abdulhamid was responsible for the military failure. Reacting to such charges, the Sultan dismissed parliament and in 1878 suspended the constitution.

The transition from Ottomanism, the view that the Turkish elements of the Ottoman Empire were Ottoman first and Turkish second, to Turkism, the view that they were Turkish first and Ottoman second, was a slow process which spanned many years. After defeat in the Great War, the collapse of the empire and the birth of the Turkish Republic, the attempt at 'purifying' the Ottoman language of Arabic words was speeded up and the change of the alphabet from

Arabic to Latin script was accomplished. This resulted in a total break with the past, leading to the alienation of generations of Turks from their history and the souring of relations with neighbouring countries. Like many other transformations that were ushered in by the First World War, the Turkish search for identity and place in the region is still on-going.

I thought again of how, at the outset of the war, Najib's biggest concern was what would replace the Ottoman Empire if it were to be dismantled. He predicted that the region would suffer under either British or German colonialism, depending on who won the war. He also feared what ambitions the Zionists might have in store for Palestine.

After his encounter with the Zoubi soldier on the way to Kufr Cana, Najib never made it to the village. Instead, he changed course and continued in the direction of Tiberias just in case the soldier was watching. He circled south of Mount Hittin, crossed Wadi al Fajjas, then rode down the low hills south of Hittin. Just before sunset he reached the top of Mount Arbel, where I had stood at the start of my quest. From there he could see the lake and town of Tiberias below him. In Najib's time this was a peaceful, attractive ancient town by the shores of the lake where a mixed population of Christians, Jews and Muslims lived. He had no way of knowing that by February 1949 the Israeli army would have destroyed 624 houses out of a total of about 670. The fact that many of these belonged to Jewish residents did not deter an army bent on the destruction of the city to prevent the return of the Arab residents who had been forced out. The city remained desolate until the 1970s, when attempts were made to modernise it. The result was a tacky centre that, despite its unique location next to the beautiful lake, is totally lacking in charm. It seems that this ancient city cannot recover from the shock of that terrible act of outright and wanton destruction.

Lower down the hill Najib could see some people camping. Their tent, made of animal hide and goat's hair, was a beautiful sight and looked so welcoming, yet Najib paused before approaching. He thought he recognised the horse of his friend Said al Tabari, so he was sure the man was there. But he wondered whether he would be taking a risk by placing himself in such an exposed position. Still, he rode down and presented himself. In the tent he found the sheikh with his cousin. They welcomed him and took him in as their guest for the night, even though they were well aware of the risk they were taking in harbouring a fugitive.

When morning came Najib wanted to leave because the tent was too close to the road. But the sheikh would not have it. 'We have already slaughtered a sheep for you,' he said. 'Eat lunch, then go.' Najib realised he had no choice. He stayed put, drank coffee and talked with his friend, risking capture as he sat in the exposed tent.

Just before noon Najib noticed a cavalry squadron of Ottoman soldiers out of Nazareth approaching the tent. Urgently the men conferred. If Najib left now the soldiers would grow suspicious when they saw a slaughtered sheep but no guest. They would assume that the guest had abandoned the meal and run to escape from them. This would create a problem for Najib's hosts. But if he stayed, Najib would be endangering his own life. The decision was his. He decided to stay.

The squadron approached the tent and split into two groups. One continued on to Tiberias; the other stopped at the tent. They were graciously met by the sheikh and his men, who took their horses and made a place for them in the tent. It was clear that some of the soldiers recognised Najib, but they kept quiet out of respect for their host. Lunch was prepared and the soldiers and Najib ate the delicious meat of the freshly slaughtered sheep and drank coffee. Before they left Sheikh Tabari's tent to catch up with the others in Tiberias, two of those who had recognised Najib approached him and whispered in his ear, 'Henceforth you're advised not to take such risks, or you'll regret it.'

It was now eighteen months since Najib had left home in Haifa. So much had happened to complicate his life. In the account he wrote of his flight he says that one of the main reasons for not wanting to go into exile was his interest in remaining close to the centre of events as a journalist. What he does not mention, however, is the fact that, a year after his departure, his wife eloped with a Turkish officer, leaving behind their three young children. The only reference he makes to this in his novelistic account is when he describes the ways he suffered during his imprisonment in Damascus for adhering to his principles, counting the violation of his honour as his worst punishment. This must have profoundly depressed him. How could he go about using his contacts with Ottoman officials to find his wife and bring her back when he was not able to show his face? And on whom could he inflict the burden of taking care of their three children? He could not leave them alone and had no money to send for their upkeep. Having considered his options, he decided to throw caution to the wind and return to Haifa. But then events took a turn to make him change his mind again.

First he got word that his friend Sheikh Wajih Zaid, to whom he had first appealed for advice in Nazareth, was travelling to the United States on a mission from the Ottoman government to try to convince the US government not to enter the war against Germany and the Ottomans. His absence was a cause of concern for Najib, who felt bereft without his friend and protector.

Then he heard that the Turkish military governor of Syria, Jamal Pasha, was being inundated with intelligence reports. Thinking they would curry favour with him by informing on fellow citizens, many people were coming forward with fabricated tales of misdeeds, leading to scores of Arab leaders being put on military trial and hanged. There was also a marked widening of the rift between Arabs and Turks in the army. Junior Turkish officers were mistreating Arab conscripts and exposing them to unnecessary danger. More and more Arabs were doing all they could to escape conscription and levels of despondency were rising significantly. Still Jamal Pasha would not heed the advice of those who pleaded with him to put an end to the policy of punishment by hanging and replace it with exile. As a result, Arab leaders who could have made a difference were eliminated. It was only in June 1916, when the Sharif of Mecca, Hussein Ibn Ali, started the Arab Revolt in collusion with the British, that Jamal Pasha seems to have realised the grave consequences of his policy of alienating Arabs. Henceforth, fewer Arabs were hanged.

While in exile in Nazareth Najib learned how he had been betrayed by someone he considered a friend. A letter had been deposited in the post office mailbox at the German Colony in Haifa containing a warning 'from the citizens of Haifa to the Ottoman Government' that unless it 'feeds the people, lifts the pressure on them and makes peace with the Allies', they would 'raise the flags of surrender next time a British ship enters Haifa's waters'. It was assumed that the letter was the work of Christians and a number of prominent Catholics were arrested. They were put on trial in a military court, but rather than hang them Jamal Pasha, in keeping with the recent change in his policy, decided to exile them to Anatolia.

Afterwards the military commander of Haifa summoned a number of the city's dignitaries. He asked them who they thought could have written this letter and put it in the mailbox. None of them would venture to confirm that this was a set-up and that those in exile were entirely innocent. To win favour, one of them said that he believed this was the work of Najib Nassar. After they left the commander's office, this man was asked why he had falsely accused Najib: 'How could you allow yourself to impugn an innocent man with such a serious offence? Isn't Najib in enough trouble as it is?' The man answered, 'What harm can come to him if we add one more offence to what he has already commited? Is he not already a fugitive?'

Even though the German consul who had originally submitted a complaint against Najib had died of typhus, there were still others who wished him ill. More accusations were reaching the ears of the Haifa commander. The order now called for Najib's apprehension dead or alive. A thorough investigation was carried out and the authorities learned of every house where Najib had taken refuge since leaving Haifa. The commander was issued with strict orders to dispatch a strong force to search every one of them. Twenty-four policemen came to Kamel Kawar's house first, but he and his son had gone into hiding to avoid conscription. In the house were Kamel's wife, Um Ameen, and a domestic helper. The police searched the house and garden thoroughly. Then they proceeded to the house of Issa al Douri, but again only the wife and small children were present. Having checked there as well, they continued their search at all the houses where Najib had been. Meanwhile Najib was hiding in a small room no further than fifty metres away from the first two places they had looked. He had moved there just before the hunt began, once Al Douri had been alerted by the local commander that if Najib was hiding in his house he should 'give him up'.

These renewed attempts to capture him made it clear to Najib that it was far too dangerous for him to remain in Nazareth. He gathered his few possessions – his *abba*, which he threw over his shoulder, and the three riyals left of the five that a generous friend had sent him – then told Um Ameen Kawar, who had been so kind to him, that he was leaving.

'Where to?' she asked.

'Wherever my God bids me go,' he replied, and walked away.

One detects in Najib's description of this episode the sense that, despite the danger he was in, he relished the fact that he had simplified his life to the greatest possible degree. All he had was the cloak on his back and a little money in his pocket. He was a romantic who wanted to live a simple life with as few possessions as possible, free of the trappings of modern life. This was why he later thought of this period, risky and dangerous as his escape was, as the happiest time in his life.

The only photograph of Najib, taken at another time, depicts a middle-aged, broad-shouldered man with thick white hair and a moustache, a full round face with fair skin, big intense eyes and the large ears characteristic of the Nassars. Perhaps especially for the occasion he had donned a three-piece suit. He was seated at his desk in deep concentration, holding a fountain pen in his hand and writing. He wore a dogged expression. This portrait must have been taken long after the ordeal of his escape. When he left Um Ameen, Najib was thin and owned very little, but by all accounts he was a happier man. Despite being pursued, with the knowledge that capture would lead to death by hanging, he still enjoyed the freedom of going where he pleased, on foot or horseback, stopping at the various Bedouin encampments and villages that dotted the hills, taking cover behind trees and rocks, having faith in himself and his ability to survive.

After leaving Nazareth, where he had many friends, Najib was no longer within reach of a town and so could not be certain of finding someone to accommodate and feed him. For the next twelve months he wandered in the wilderness, his living conditions becoming more difficult once he crossed to the eastern bank of the River Jordan, where he found himself living the kind of life a man of his class and background rarely experienced.

Najib walked first to A'yn Mahel, where he was offered food at a friend's house, then to the Subeih forest and from there to the village of Dabburiya at the foot of Mount Tabor.

It was already dark when he entered the house of Tawfiq, from the well-known Fahhoum family, who was suffering from malaria. After they had eaten dinner, the man claimed that he was about to leave for Nazareth to get treatment. However, Najib knew this was not true and that Tawfiq Fahhoum was in fact worried that the Ottoman police might come that night and find Najib with him. But he could not bring himself to ask Najib to leave. This was why he preferred not to be home when the soldiers came. There were not many occasions when Najib spoke badly of anyone but this was one of them. In his account of the encounter, Najib's self-righteous side comes across. He refuses to take into account the danger to which his host was exposing himself by accommodating a fugitive like him. After berating the cowardice of Tawfiq Fahhoum, Najib writes that he felt it would be too risky to be out at night and so decided to stay instead with a builder who lived nearby, a simple man under whose roof he had a good sleep. In the morning he continued on his way to the village of A'yn Doar.

A few years earlier he had published a story in his newspaper, *Al Karmil*, about the unruly nature of this village and how the Ottoman authorities could not succeed in making any arrests there. He had compared it to the Hauran region, in the north-west, where the Druze community had carried out a successful rebellion against the Ottoman government and managed to live in relative autonomy. As he walked towards the village, Najib wondered whether Abdullah Fahhoum, to whose house he was heading, might hand him over to the authorities in retaliation for what he had written about the village. Instead he was given a warm welcome. As it turned out the man adhered too strongly to the ideal of hospitality to turn him in.

It is always the case that Najib is forthright and honest, never concealing anything he does and never intending to deceive anyone. He makes his case through the mouth of this man who should be an enemy because of what Najib had written about the village.

Najib told his host everything that had happened to him. When he had finished, Abdullah said that he had heard all the rumours circulating about him. 'The authorities believe you favour the English because you repeated many times that it would be better for the Ottomans to align themselves with them. Your vehement criticism of the Germans has aroused strong feelings against you as well. You also wrote damning things against Emir Shakib, who came to Jerusalem to preach the cause of the Axis powers. All this has allowed your enemies to portray you to Jamal Pasha as someone who loves the English and is a spy and an enemy of the coalition Axis powers. So they have vowed to pursue you until they capture and hang you as they have done to others before you.'

'What do you think I should do now?' Najib asked Abdullah.

'Wait here a few days. No one will suspect that I would harbour you, because people know how fiercely you have vilified me.'

That day a large contingent of police came to the village looking for Najib. Abdullah welcomed them, offering food and coffee. Their leader described how the search for Najib had been going on for many days now and how furious his commander was that they were still unable to find him. More police were being recruited for the job and would be sent to different areas.

'It has fallen to us,' said the man, 'to search here. When we passed by Dabburiya we were told that a stranger had been seen approaching the house of Tawfiq Bey and was seen again leaving it in the morning. The description fitted Najib.'

On hearing this, Abduallah told the police, 'If only you knew how much I despise this man. He has done me a lot of harm – said terrible things and incited the government against me. If I could find him I would carry him between my teeth and bring him to Jamal Pasha to get my revenge.'

'You have not heard his news, then?' one policeman asked. 'Has no one mentioned that he passed near here today?'

'Had I heard this I would have been in pursuit of him myself and you would not have found me at home.'

'But have you not heard that he has been hiding in Nazareth? Your brother Abdul Hamid knows this. Did he not tell you?'

'My brother is a friend of Najib's, but he knows how violently I hate the man. This is why he didn't mention the news to me. I promise you that should I hear anything I will be the first to go after him and capture him for you.'

All this reassured the police. They removed their cartridge belts, lay down and immediately fell asleep. But Abdullah was worried that if they rested now they would stay up all night and continue with their search. So he roused them from their slumber.

'Those like you who are instructed with carrying out such an important mission must stay up. Shall we put our heads together?'

They sat up, rubbing their sleepy eyes and pleading that they only wanted to rest for an hour, so that they could wake refreshed and resume their search.

Abdullah told them that they would not find Najib 'even if he was in the same house … because people seem to like Najib very much. I myself can't understand why. They will not give him up. But I can go and secretly sniff around the villages, find him and bring him back to you. I want to go with you to deliver him, lest some people stop you on the way and try to take him away from you.'

The police stayed at Abdullah's house and the servants were instructed to feed them and give them coffee and cigarettes until evening. The elders of the village came over and they all had dinner with the police.

Abdullah made it clear to them that they were welcome to sleep in his house, but, he said, 'My family and guests are too numerous. You might be more comfortable sleeping where you can get up early to continue with your search. I will take you over to the house of the *mukhtar*, who will put you up.'

They all walked over to the *mukhtar*'s, then after spending some time there to see them comfortably settled Abdullah rushed back to his house, found Najib hiding, fed him and suggested that they ride together away from the village.

'Have you decided where you're headed?' he asked Najib.

'Yes, I have. To the village of Tireh. If you would accompany me to Wadi al Bira, below the hill where the village stands, I will then be able to manage on my own.'

Abdullah found two horses, which he insisted on saddling himself because he did not want others to be involved, and without delay the two men rode together under cover of darkness so that Abdullah could be back before daybreak. Before he left him, Abdullah asked Najib whether he had any money. Najib remained silent, too proud to admit that he had none. Abdullah dug into his pocket, found two gold riyals and gave them to him.

The village of Tireh sits on a gently sloping hill overlooking the sharp inclines of Wadi al Bira. To reach it Penny and I started to walk from the entrance to the nature reserve two-thirds of the way up to Kawkab al Hawa and the fortress of Belvoir. The signpost read in English 'Nahal Taver Nature Reserve' and in Arabic 'Mahmiet Wadi al Bira (Wadi al Tavor)'.

The hill from which we started was steep. From below Kawkab the eastern side of the Jordan opened up and I could see the continuation of the valley through the hills on the other side. The wind rose as it funnelled through the meandering wadi. When I looked down I could see how it continued north-west to Mount Tabor and east to the River Jordan. It was the natural passageway between the hills to get to the River Jordan and across it to the East Bank. The spring flowers had withered. Without the greenery, the hills looked more spacious and golden but it seemed as if there was nothing between earth and sky. The heat appeared to rise directly from the ground. Only the most hardy and drought-resistant bushes remained, together with pink bindweed and blue globe thistles rising from the dry yellow grass. Brown limestone rocks lay exposed on the sides of the hill. Some were graced by the prostrate caper shrubs, which seem to grow without any water and produce lovely fan-like pink flowers. These open valleys with cavernous hills at their sides are so unlike those in the central parts of the country. The path that we took meandered, gently riding the hills, although at times passing close to the edge of cliffs, with rocks shearing away to sharp drops. Throughout the trek Mount Tabor continued to dominate the scene, standing in the distance like a benevolent presence watching over the mouth of this wadi. A wondrously strange mount indeed.

The plateau of Galilee, where we now were, is a continuation of the Lebanon mountains to the north, where the average height ranges between 300 and 600 metres. The precipitous cliffs, deep ravines and rocky slopes of Lebanon are replaced here by low rounded hills, smooth outlines and grass-covered uplands, which, as Lawrence noted, are reminiscent of some parts of the English Pennines. This Lebano-Galilean massif comes to a somewhat abrupt end at the plain of Marj Ibn Amer, which is described by geologists as a tectonic trough formed by subsidence of sediments along fault lines. Mount Tabor interrupts the sweep of the plain on the south-east. This is why it stands out and looks more like a mound than a hill, sitting so gracefully and comfortably claiming for itself a unique position at the end of the valley. It resembles the man-made pyramids in the Egyptian desert, looking out for the wadi and protecting those travelling in it. Only when you climb its summit do you realise how high it is. From its top the whole area stretches out before you, giving the impression that you are viewing it from a high-flying aeroplane.

As we approached the stream in the wadi the croaking of the frogs grew louder and I could hear the cooing of partridges and pigeons. Close to the water the ruin of a citadel stands sentinel. There was no sign identifying it. Someone had scrawled in blue paint the word *shalom* (peace) in Hebrew letters. I climbed up and saw a hole drilled in the tower-like structure which I assumed must have been for fixing a mast or banner. Between this tower and the wadi was a cistern enclosed by the remains of a wall at a lower level than the ground around it. Could this have been an Ottoman fort with a cistern to provide water for those manning it when the stream dried up? If so Najib would certainly have avoided this spot.

We continued walking in a north-westerly direction. The wadi meandered and narrowed. In most parts it was exposed, so that it would not conceal a rider along its bank. The hills to the west were higher than those to the east. By the water was a good riding trail. We walked on a dirt track used by four-wheel-drive vehicles. Along the western slopes I could see almond trees, which I had learned to assume marked the locations on the hill where Arab villages had once stood.

I looked up at the hills. They were different from those around Ramallah, much more fertile, with richer, deeper soil and fewer stones. They sloped gently towards the wadi, descending more like a slightly swelling wave than a turbulent crashing one, as is the case in our hills. They were much less precipitous and didn't seem to need terracing to preserve the soil from erosion. The hills around this reserve were not cultivated. They were used as grazing land for cattle. The sheep and goats belonging to the Arabs who had once grazed their flocks there were gone, along with their owners.

A sign pointed the way to A'yn Shahal, the Hebrew name of A'yn al Baida. This was the spring used by the villagers of Tireh. But we did not make it there. Just as we approached it we encountered a herd of cows and bulls belonging to an Israeli dairy farm, Tnuvah, lined up by the gate. It was the mating season.

'I'm from Illinois,' Penny reminded me. 'I know about the danger of approaching mating bovines.'

Mating or not, Penny has a phobia of cows. She once read that a bull gored to death a hiker in Scotland. I wanted to see what was left of the village of Tireh, whose inhabitants had been forced out on 15 April 1948, but the way these oversized bulls, with their long sharp horns, were eying us was far too menacing even for a determined explorer like me. We decided to turn back. When we got to the fort we stopped just behind it, took off our shoes and socks and dangled our bare feet in the cold water. Damselflies, with their blue gossamer wings with the single black spot, rather like a Japanese painting, hopped on the water. I wondered whether Najib had done the same at some point in his journey to relax his nerves after the stress and anxiety of the chase.

He had no luggage as he walked alone up the hill after Abduallah left him, only the *abba* that was slung over his shoulder. He got to the house of Sheikh Mustafa al Khatib just before dawn. The morning sun began to light up the hill. He could hear the cock crowing and smell the familiar fragrance of a farmhouse, the embers of the fire from the evening before doused with water and the droppings of chickens and goats. As he approached, the dogs began to bark but no one was up to meet him. He got to the door and began to knock, softly at first, then more loudly when he got no response. Eventually he heard someone rushing to the door.

The sheikh opened the door, saw Najib and said, 'I thought it was the army. What brings you here so early in the morning?'

'It's a long story,' Najib replied.

Coffee was brewed and soon freshly baked bread was served. Najib and the sheikh shared a breakfast of olives, yoghurt, for which the village was famous, and bread. After they had eaten and sipped their coffee Najib told the sheikh the whole story, only omitting the part about how Abdullah had brought him to the village.

Najib then asked the sheikh whether his son could get a horse ready and accompany him on foot to Wadi al Bira. 'From there I will continue on foot,' he added.

'Why?' asked the sheikh. 'My son can take you wherever you're going.'

'I don't want your son to know where I'm going. I don't want him implicated, in case he is stopped and interrogated.'

Soon the horse was ready and Najib rode to the mouth of the wadi, gave back the horse to the sheikh's son and continued on foot. He had been walking for half an hour when he met Sheikh Assad Fahhoum riding and inspecting his crops in the wadi. Najib called out to him.

At first the sheikh did not recognise Najib, but when he did he stopped, dismounted and asked, 'What brings you all this way on foot?'

'Don't ask where I come from or how I came. All I can say is Jamal Pasha is ever more determined to capture me and I am going into hiding.'

The sheikh put Najib on his horse and told him, 'I will take the first horse we come across.'

It was only minutes before a Bedouin was seen approaching on horseback. Sheikh Assad asked the man to give him his horse, promising that he would return it that evening.

The picture that emerges from Najib's description is one of great trust and generosity among the people of the Galilee. There was no question of refusing or arguing against this demand. The sheikh didn't need to do more than promise. The Bedouin's is an oral culture, highly regulated by conventions. The sheikh from a nearby village is respected and obeyed without question. The Bedouin obliged. The two men rode through the wadi and forded the River Jordan at Al Makhada. Then they continued into the wilderness of what is now the Hashemite Kingdom of Jordan, where Najib was once again seeking refuge from the Ottoman soldiers pursuing him.

It was also time for me, in my pursuit of this renegade relative, to cross the river. In 2008, though the physical distance had not changed and the torrential river had dwindled to a shallow stream, crossing it had become a much more complicated affair.

6

Hur Hur, Hau Hau

The young man who picked me up on the Jordanian side of the Allenby Bridge to drive me to my hotel in Amman had a deeply lined face and looked older than his years. For much of his working life he had driven his taxi on the forty-five-kilometre-long steep and winding road between the city and the bridge. We talked along the way and he told me that his family came from Ramleh, an ancient Palestinian town close to the Mediterranean Sea. After they were forced out during the 1948 Nakba, some went to Jordan, others to Lebanon. His maternal uncle still lives in Nablus, but he has never visited any part of the country west of the river. Everyday he parks just one kilometre away from the Allenby Bridge, picks up visitors from the land beyond and drives them to Amman. When I asked why he had never visited the West Bank when it was part of Jordan, he said he was born in 1968, a year after the Israeli occupation.

'Why not come for a visit?' I asked.

'A couple of times I applied for a permit from Israel but was refused. I have many cousins in Nablus whom I've never met.'

'What do they do?' I asked.

'They have a dairy factory in Nablus. They say it's near the traffic circle in the centre. I hear them speak about the circle but I don't know what it is.' Then he asked me, 'How far is the sea from where you live in Ramallah?'

I told him in normal times it is only a forty-minute drive. Now with the roadblocks and the wall it takes much longer.

'Do you think you'll ever visit Palestine?' I asked.

'I don't think so. I have no hope the conflict will be resolved in my lifetime,' he replied.

In 1992 I was involved in the much-heralded negotiations that were taking place for the first time between Israel and the Palestinians in Washington, DC. We would cross the bridge to take the plane to the US full of hope that we were working for a negotiated settlement that would end the conflict. I'll never forget the look on the faces of the PLO drivers who took me from Amman Airport to the bridge. How they would linger at the furthest point they were permitted to go, trying to extend for as long as possible the experience of looking at the unreachable land. They would then follow me with their gaze as I walked into the territory forbidden to them, longing to accompany me on the journey home they could not make. They didn't say anything but in their eyes was that yearning to cross back to the land from which their families came and to which they've never been allowed to return, not even for a visit. The prospects for peace had rekindled their hope that this might yet happen. Such experiences motivated me to work as hard as I could on the task at hand. In 1993, when the Declaration of Principles was signed between Israel and the PLO, some Palestinians were allowed back, first to Jericho and Gaza, then to the rest of the West Bank. Now most are confined in the West Bank or the Gaza Strip, unable to travel beyond these tiny regions, not even for a visit to the villages in Israel from which their parents had been forced to flee.

When I turned to look at my driver's unsmiling face his gaze was fixed on the road. I stared at the mountains across the Dead Sea. They looked more formidable than they had ever appeared to me: an impregnable wall of rose-coloured stone, lit up by the strong noon sun, blocking the land of Palestine beyond.

I was tempted to advise the driver to look with new eyes at his surroundings as he worked his route. Perhaps it would brighten his outlook to think of the scene as part of a long rift extending across continents, a sweep of deep-set lands, lakes and valleys, a natural wonder of our amazing planet that has survived and will continue to exist beyond the borders people and political entities impose to confine us. I knew that this way of looking and thinking had helped me overcome the restrictive, depressing conditions created by our dismal political realities. But turning again to look at his sombre face, I saw how deeply etched were the two lines on both sides of it and was dissuaded from trying to get into such a conversation with him.

The urban sprawl of Amman is impressive. From a small town in the 1920s, it has developed into a city of close to a million people. In 1922 the whole of Transjordan had a population of 225,000, of whom 103,000 were nomads. Before 1948, many of the young Bedouins used to cross the river to Haifa to work as day labourers at the port or in factories. Their flocks of sheep and goats moved across the eastern and western banks of the river wherever vegetation could be found. They had no

1. This is the only known photo of Najib. With pen in hand, he has a dogged expression that suggests absolute focus.

2. Najib married Sadhij in 1929. One of the most militant leaders of the women's movement in Palestine, Sadhij was described by the British authorities as a 'very dangerous woman'.

3. This is the only family portrait that survives, which my grandmother displayed on the table in the vestibule of her home in Ramallah. Katbeh (right), sits on the edge of her chair ready to leap up and go back to her kitchen. Her husband Ibrahim, Najib's brother, wears a three-piece suit, lending him an air of great authority. My grandmother, Julia, stands with a fashion model's pose, her right leg elegantly extended.

4. Bedouin tribes offered vital help to Najib over ninety years ago. They provided him with shelter and fed him the milk and cheeses for which they were famous.

5. Haifa in Najib's time was a cluster of residences and public buildings tucked between the narrow central stretch of seashore and the mountain slopes west of the bay and east of the Carmel promontory, though a few isolated buildings sprung up outside these valleys, such as Rashid's house (Najib's brother) on Mount Carmel.

6 & 7. Tiberias, c. 1911: this was a peaceful, attractive, ancient town by the shores of the lake where a mixed population of Christians, Jews and Muslims lived. It remained desolate until the 1970s, when attempts were made to modernise it. The result was a tacky centre that, despite its unique location, is totally lacking in charm. The once predominant black and white stone buildings now stand out painfully. The new town is almost entirely Jewish.

8. The Jordan is a fast-flowing river, one without a permanent course. It constantly twists and turns, luxuriating in the deep green valley through which it surges. It covers a linear distance of about 100 kilometres but it winds through more than 200 kilometres on its journey, falling to 400 metres below sea level at the Dead Sea. Not surprising, then, that the Jordan is the only river in the region with no major city on its banks.

9 & 10. It is refreshing to think how, in the course of his flight from Ottoman soldiers, Najib was able to cross the river and reach the eastern bank without the need for visas or permits. He did so on horseback, at a place called Al Makhada (the ford in the river). The top photograph shows an expedition from the Palestinian Exploration Fund (PEF) crossing the ford in 1897. The bottom photograph is the Allenby Bridge, constructed over the original ford in 1918, but which was bombed on 8 June 1967. The image show refugees fleeing across the crumbling remains to Jordan itself.

11. Many of the Arab villages and Bedouin encampments that thrived in Najib's time have since been removed and new Israeli villages established where they once stood. Only from photographs, such as this of A'yn Doar, do I know the landscape as it had once been. Najib had been welcomed in Ayn Doar by Abdullah Fahhoum during his exile.

12. The fertile Bekaa plains, part of the Rift Valley, that stretches far and long, north to Turkey and south to the Red Sea and into Africa, utterly oblivious of the man-made borders that come and go.

13. The Ottomans constructed roads between main urban centres and railway lines that connected the far-flung parts of the empire. This photograph shows the prized Haifa–Damascus railroad in construction. The tracks stop just outside the Al Buss Palestinian Refugee site; the train that could once have taken refugees home has long stopped running.

4. Alongside the Al Buss refugee site is the Al-Bass Archeological Site, declared a UNESCO world heritage location in 1984. It has the largest and best preserved Roman ippodrome in the world. A strange juxtaposition of ancient and new.

15. My great grandfather originally came from Ayn Anoub. Perhaps he even attended the school in this picture. During the Tanzimat (literally 'reorganisation') period in the nineteenth century the Ottomans brought about impressive administrative reforms, including the building of schools and hospitals.

16. I returned to Ayn Anoub in 2010 to search for any trace of my great grandfather's family. From the roof of the school, the scenic bay of Beirut stretched below us, a beautiful vista of the city and the sea. With its perfect bay, Beirut reminded me of Haifa. The similarity must have helped Najib feel at home there.

sense of national allegiance. They thought of themselves first and foremost as members of their tribe.

What is now recognised as the Hashemite Kingdom of Jordan was created through the efforts of Emir Abdullah, one of the sons of Hussein Ibn Ali, who as Najib was fleeing the Ottoman police was fighting alongside the Allied forces to bring down Ottoman rule in the eastern Mediterranean. An ambitious man, Abdullah had set his eyes on the throne of Iraq. Receiving no encouragement from the British to pursue this objective, he set off from the city of Medina in the Hijaz at the head of a force of nearly 2,000 men, arriving in November 1920 in Ma'an, a small village in northern Jordan. There he revealed his intention of marching on Damascus and driving out the French to Captain Alex Kirkbride. This quick-witted British officer, having received no instructions on how to deal with Abdullah, decided to welcome him in the name of the National Government of Moab. Abdullah wanted to know whether 'the National Government of Moab had ever been recognised internationally', to which Kirkbride replied unflinchingly, 'I am not quite sure of its international status. I feel, however, that the question is largely of an academic nature now that Your Highness is here.'

Once Abdullah set up his headquarters in Amman, the British discussed whether or not to eject him from Transjordan and administer the area directly. T. E. Lawrence, Winston Churchill's adviser on Arab affairs, was of the opinion that anti-Zionist sentiment in Palestine would wane and that Transjordan could be turned into a safe haven for displaced Palestinians by appointing a ruler on whom Britain could bring pressure to bear to check anti-Zionist agitation. The ideal, said Lawrence, would be 'a person who was not too powerful, and who was not an inhabitant of Transjordan, but who relied on His Majesty's Government for the retention of his office'. Kirkbride later wrote that Transjordan was meant to be used as a reservation on which to resettle Arabs once the national home for the Jews in Palestine had become an accomplished fact.

And so it has been for the millions of Palestinians whom Israel succeeded in uprooting in the course of its many wars. Now well over half of Jordan's population is Palestinian. By imposing severe restrictions on Palestinian life and economy, Israel continues to attempt to drive more Palestinians out of the land it has occupied. Many of its leaders have repeatedly mortified the Hashemite regime by claiming that Jordan is Palestine. But for the heavily secured borders, many more Palestinians might have moved to Jordan. The well-to-do Palestinians in Jordan are mainly professionals and merchants. The civil service and armed forces are almost exclusively staffed by Jordanians.

The normally tranquil surface of relations between the two groups is betrayed by reference to Palestinian Jordanians as Baljikiyyah, meaning Belgians, which is intended to denationalise Palestinian Jordanians by rendering them foreign. The origin of this anti-Palestinian epithet is not clear. It might be in reference to the Belgian-made military boots and fatigues worn by the Palestinian guerrillas when they operated from Jordan before the civil war broke out in 1970 which distinguished them from the US-equipped Jordanian army. Another arena where divisions between the two groups can flare up is the football stadium. Whether support is given to the Wihdat or the Ramtha team becomes a national act of loyalty to one's Palestinianness or Jordanianness respectively. Matches often occasion Palestinian protests and assertions of national identity. Fights can break out between the fans, leading to police intervention and arrests. Tempers can get so strained that Jordanians might call on the Israeli Minister of Defence, as they recently beseeched Ehud Barak, to strike the Palestinians more severely; some even called upon the Jordanian King Abdullah to divorce his Palestinian wife.

I've never been fond of Amman, always thinking it was a city without a soul, well organised and clean yet sterile, too highly policed and unexciting. I was determined to spend as brief a time in the city as possible. So next morning I found a driver to take me north to the land where Najib spent the last part of his flight from the Ottoman authorities. Abu Ahmad was dressed in a dark suit. He had intense eyes, a mouth pursed because of the number of missing teeth, and a prominent chin. I took an immediate liking to this man. He had a friendly demeanour and seemed open to adventure.

I wanted him to drive along the river so I could observe the terrain I am familiar with from the other side of the border. But much of this area was restricted and we ended up driving over the hills, along the eastern side of the Rift Valley. The land east of the river is part of a different tectonic plate from the one making up the western bank. The northern half of Jordan forms an irregular plateau lying at an altitude from 300 to 600 metres. West of this, towards the Jordan Valley, the landscape is open and rolling, with level stretches and broad valleys interspersed with occasional basaltic ridges, some of which reach 900 metres in height. In Najib's time the eastern plateau along with southern Syria constituted a single administrative unit called the Hauran. Much of the land in northern Jordan is buried under igneous matter. With a good water supply it can be extremely productive, since the soil is very fertile, being derived from lava formed by a relatively recent upwelling in the fractured edge of the Arabian plate. In Roman times the Hauran was one of the main granaries of the empire. As we climbed up these impressive ridges, occasionally driving down into the broad valleys, Abu Ahmad told me about his life.

'I have been a driver for fifty-four years,' he said. 'I began in 1955. I am close to seventy now. Never been to a doctor. Every day I wake up I think it a blessing to be alive. I never worry or make calculations. If I have a dinar in my pocket to buy a sandwich I'm satisfied. If I have five dinars in my pocket I feel rich. I waste no time on following financial markets, as many of my customers do on their mobile phones. Life used to be hard when I was growing up, but people were closer together, their hearts were open, not like today. After the Nakba there was hunger, real hunger. We had very little to eat and no work. I come from the village of Balata, near Nablus, but I had to leave to seek work. I came to Amman in 1955 and began working as a taxi driver. In the past people lived next to each other and everyone knew what everyone else did. Now the city has grown and people live apart and are alienated from each other.

'My schooling stopped at the fourth grade. We studied Morris Books numbers one and two. But I've retained everything I studied. Once I was bringing back university students from Damascus. I asked them, "How many letters are there in the English alphabet?" They hesitated, then said, "Twenty-four." I said, "Wrong! Twenty-six", and I recited them: A, B, C ... They were impressed. They didn't deserve the diplomas they were getting. It was different when I was growing up. We had respect for our teachers. We studied by the light of a candle, but we had to learn everything we were given. If we went to class and did not recite everything we studied the day before we were given the *falaga*. The teacher had a pomegranate wood cane and would rap us on the knuckles with it. We were not like today's students who smoke in class in front of their teachers.'

Whenever he passed Jordanian police or soldiers Abu Ahmad would greet them in a loud voice: '*Marhaba,*

hukoumeh!' ('Hello, government!') Some of the policemen
at whom he shouted this greeting did not like it, suspecting
that perhaps he was poking fun at them. But what could they
say: 'We're not *hukoumeh*'? When they stooped down to face
him, their angry look would be met by Abu Ahmad's bright,
cheerful face and this would deter them from penalising him.
When on occasion he was asked to open the luggage compart-
ment, he would spring out of the car with alacrity. He was a
wiry man with quick movements. When I first met him he
was behind the driver's seat. Now that I saw him standing up,
I realised how short he was. He was a survivor, the quintessential Palestinian, aware of his strength and depending only
on himself, never expecting help from any governmental
agency. All he wanted of the *hukoumeh* was that it keep off
his back. Like many a Palestinian, his veneer of amiability
concealed deep anger. It came through when he spoke of what
he had left behind in Palestine and the land his family owned,
which was now settled by a Saba'wi (someone from Bir es
Sabeeh-Beersheba).

'An Arab?' I asked, stupidly wondering if he was perhaps
a collaborator.

'No. Jewish of course,' he said.

Abu Ahmad must have decided I was a tense person and
likely to get an ulcer, so he began giving me remedies. It was
a kind thing to do. 'Honey,' he said, 'is best for ulcers. And
an onion or two, possibly with two cloves of garlic, at lunch
would prevent heart attacks. Figs are good for the stomach.
So are prickly pears. Their seeds purify the passages of the
stomach. It is better to eat spinach, beans and cauliflower than
meat, chicken or fish. These days they feed animals too many
chemicals to fatten them and make them grow fast. It is good
to start the day with *zait* and *zaiter* [olive oil and thyme].
What did we have to eat in the village? Bread smeared with

olive oil, that was the staple food. And people lived to their nineties. We *fellaheen* never saw a doctor. There weren't any nearby. But we have our remedies. If a child gets sick in the village his mother would know what to do. Where I grew up we had many snakes. If anyone got bitten they grabbed a rooster, placed his rear end right on the wound and it sucked up all the poison. The cock died and the child was saved.'

From his description of his life I could surmise that he had not lived in a village for many years and yet he continued to refer to 'we *fellaheen*'. As he gave me more health tips I looked at his hands clutching the steering wheel. They were rough like those of a farmer's. The village of Balata, from where he came, is now a suburb of Nablus and famous for its large refugee camp. I asked him when was the last time he went there for a visit? Nineteen seventy-four.

'I have a brother who lives in Nablus who is not allowed by Israel to travel out of the Occupied Territories. It has now become difficult for me to get a visa from Israel to visit him. I wouldn't know my nephews if I met them in the street. I have another brother in Venezuela who is also out of touch. He married and settled there. I provided all my sons with an education. One is the head of a department in the Arab Bank, another in the Cairo Amman Bank, and a third is still at university. Education is a treasure.'

How often one heard similar sentiments expressed by Palestinians.

'If you have education,' Abu Ahmad went on, 'you can make it in the world. If they want to get married or acquire an apartment, this is their business. Our country is gone. Palestine will never return. I've given up on the Arab states. They are like beads in a rosary: when one slips away the rest follow.'

Abu Ahmad continued to stop along the way and ask for

directions. 'It isn't shameful to ask,' he would say. 'If one is not sure, better ask.'

But there were few men around to ask in these villages. Only the women seemed to stay in the houses. Abu Ahmad explained that all the men in this part of the country work in the military or the civil service. They leave for the week and return home for the weekend. The villages looked abandoned. There was no agriculture in evidence. They all lived off the government.

The villages that we passed were spread out, with one-storey houses surrounded by large gardens, only a few of which were tended. What was outstanding about these villages was how uncramped they were. They reminded me of the villages on our side some twenty-five years ago, before the Israeli military authorities began imposing their policy of strangulation, drawing plans that limited the villages to existing built-up areas, declaring those limits the boundaries of the village for the next four decades, preventing future expansion and forcing villagers to build upwards, thereby spoiling the charm of these hitherto unobtrusive settlements nestling among the slopes of the ancient hills. Though spread out, the villages here looked drab. In the small area of culti-vable land allowed them, Palestinians would grow gardens with a splash of colour from bougainvillea or geranium, both drought-resistant plants. I doubt that the villagers were aware of the privilege of not having the same sorts of restriction placed on their enjoyment of their land and their right to expand as are imposed on the Palestinians.

Most people here belonged to large clans. All the men knew to which clan they belonged and these ties were preserved throughout their lives. They meticulously observed tribal traditions and maintained cordial relations with their clansmen. Rituals abound whether for happy occasions, such as feast days, weddings or the birth of a new male child, or sad, such as deaths or injuries as a result of a feud. A member of a clan has no alternative but to stand with his clan at such times. It is not unusual for the free time of an adult male in traditional societies like this to be entirely consumed in fulfilling social obligations, when he is not expected to do much more than sit around in order to augment the presence of the men on his side. Examining the faces of those we met, I could not tell whether they were happy, free as they were of the oppression we were subjected to under occupation. But it seemed they could not cherish and be glad about what they took for granted. It is easy for us to lament what we don't have, harder for others to appreciate the misery and suffering they are spared.

Historically, Palestine was the more developed area, the more fertile, the more progressive and culturally diverse. The inhabitants of the east bank of the river used to plant grain, raise goats and sheep and sell these to the people on the west bank of the river. When Najib crossed to the eastern side it was like going into the wilderness. Jordan has come a long way since then.

Najib had heard that the soldiers were getting closer in their search. They were under strict orders to get him. He had to go across.

After fording the river, he and his companion, Sheikh Assad, headed to the tent camp of Ali Shamali (someone coming from the north), where they found him in a *murab'a* (a square tent). They were welcomed and served coffee, then Ali, an old man with bad eyesight, turned to the sheikh and asked, 'Who do you have with you?'

'This is Najib Nassar.'

The old man called to an attendant and Najib saw the man

taking a horse and leaving. He knew he was going to slaughter a sheep to feed the guests.

Najib rose and called after the man to stop, then addressed Ali: 'I have something important to tell you. Let the man stop until you hear me out.'

Najib proceeded to reveal to Ali that he was a fugitive and that Jamal Pasha had issued a warrant for his arrest. 'If you slaughter a sheep for me people around are bound to wonder who your guest might be. This can only bring me trouble. I would rather be treated as a perfectly ordinary person.'

At this point Ali beckoned the attendant and told him not to go. He then took Najib's hand and the two men walked along the bank of the River Jordan while Najib recounted the story of his escape to date. When he finished he turned to Ali. 'Now you know everything. I have come seeking refuge and would like to stay with you for a number of days, but if you are concerned that my presence might cause you hardship tell me frankly and I will find another shelter.'

Ali turned to Najib. 'Would I ever forget the great service you rendered me? Were you not the one who alerted us about the Asfar project? Had it not been for your warning, these lands on which we live would have been sold and we would be landless. You campaigned against the government selling these lands and helped us retain our rights over them.'

These were the Mudawara lands, which had been registered in the name of the Ottoman Sultan for protection. In the first decade of the twentieth century he was determined to put them on the market. This would have meant that those Bedouins who lived off the land and claimed it as their own would not have been allowed to remain on it. Najib informed them of the impending sale and agitated through his paper against it. The land ended up being registered in the names of those living on it.

'Were it not for you,' Ali added, 'we would not be here. How could we not protect you and guard you against injustice?'

I wanted to get close to the river and walk along its bank, as Najib and Ali had done. But it was all a closed military zone. My only option was to take an organised tour to the little island that is situated between the two branches of the River Jordan before they meet again and is cynically called Wahat es Salaam (Oasis of Peace), one of those infuriating joint Israeli-Jordanian projects that give peace a bad name.

We rode in the van with old women taken by their sons on an outing. Most were so decrepit that they were barely able to climb the high steps of the van. I wondered who they might be. They didn't look like tourists interested in military history or in visiting the site of the battle that took place here in 1948. Nor did they seem to be women interested in the public relations objective behind this 'oasis' of bringing the warring sides together. So I asked one of them. She told me she came from the village of Lubya in the Galilee and had been living in the Shatila Refugee Camp in Lebanon since the Nakba. She had come to Jordan in order to make this short excursion.

'Before 1967 I used to travel to Syria to stand on the Golan Heights,' she said, 'and from there I would look down at the Galilee hills to see what was happening to our land. For many years after we were forced out, the old habits would not die. When I woke up in the morning I could feel my knees jerk, ready to go out to the field and start planting, picking or weeding. But where could I go in the camp, with its narrow lanes and not enough land to plant a bed of mint? With the Israeli occupation of the Golan, it's been forty-two years now since I've been able to set eyes on those beautiful hills where

I once lived. I didn't want to die before seeing them again. So my son, God preserve him and give him strength, promised to bring me here. He said this is the closest one can get to the Galilee.'

I noticed how keenly she looked, not at what the young soldier was describing in a booming voice but across the river to the other side, the side she has not been allowed to visit for over sixty years.

This tense young soldier acted as our guide, repeating in an authoritative military voice what he had been instructed to say about the heroic feats of the Jordanian army in saving this area in the battle of 1948, concluding with how war and violence have now ended and it is time to make peace with our enemies. The passengers in the van sat in silence. We were quickly whisked around without being allowed to leave our seats. I looked at what these old men and women were seeing now and tried to compare it with what they must hold in their memories. The Israeli Galilee of today is a much changed place from the one they knew. Of the thirty-three Arab villages formerly in the sub-district of Tiberias, only four remain. All the others had been destroyed and new Israeli villages, designed to make the area look European, with red-tile roofed houses and green lawns, were put in their place. The Huleh, which they would have known as a vast marsh covering 6,000 hectares, had been drained. It had been an ecological treasure chest, with eighteen species of fish, the greatest concentration of aquatic plants in the entire Middle East and scores of species of migratory birds. Its destruction caused a deterioration in the quality of the water in Lake Tiberias, because it removed an essential 'nutrient sink' that absorbed much of the nitrogen and phosphorus from the surface run-off into the lake, where much of the rich, newly exposed and nitrified organic peat was washed down. It was also where the Marsh

Arabs lived with their water buffaloes among the papyrus reeds. Their way of life was entirely destroyed.

All that was left now was a small lake covering 240 hectares, a part of the Huleh Nature Reserve. But this event did not make it into the geography books of the Arabs living in the West Bank and Jordan, a short distance away. For years we were taught that the Galilee had two large lakes, Tiberias and Huleh.

The project of draining the marsh, undertaken in the early 1950s, gratified the young Israeli state's anachronistic urge to control nature and enabled it to claim that it was bringing civilisation to a wild and untamed region by draining malarial swamps and preserving the health of the population of the area from disease. In fact this had already been achieved in 1946, two years before the establishment of the state, when DDT was introduced. As to the thousands of hectares of rich farmland that were made available as a consequence of draining the marsh, these had little meaning for a country that, after forcing out most of the Arab population and taking over their agricultural land, was sparsely populated. The Visitors Centre has a photographic exhibition and a collection of stuffed specimens of those mammals and birds that once inhabited the marsh and have now vanished, along with the Marsh Arabs of Palestine. It also shows an agonised film that, while extolling Israel's 'great' engineering achievement, laments the environmental disaster that this has unleashed. The film's narrator tries to comfort the viewer by saying that what Israel did in the early 1950s would have happened anyway several hundreds of thousands of years later.

The goats and sheep that once roamed the Galilee hills have been replaced by the more lumbering grain-fed cows whose fabled flatulence sends into the atmosphere the carbon dioxide so harmful to our planet. The old mixed town of

Tiberias that my fellow passengers knew has mostly been destroyed. The mosque at the centre has gone except for the minaret, which stands forlornly alone, surrounded by ugly cement shopping malls and hotels that look like dormitories, devoid of any charm. The once predominant black and white stone buildings now stand out for their uniqueness. The new town is almost entirely Jewish. The water in the lake is over-pumped to serve extensive heavily water-dependent farming that makes no sense in a country with limited water resources. A number of economically unsuccessful new towns have been established in the area, isolated from the natural continuation of the land to the south by the infamous semi-permeable wall, erected to separate them from the West Bank, that prevents Palestinians from crossing over but allows Israelis living on both sides to go back and forth. Still, the hills remain as attractive as ever. Most of the trees planted before the Nakba are still there, and those strangely shaped limestone rocks, so friable that they have weeds growing in clumps all along their sides, decorate the land.

I could see the Israeli cars on the Jericho–Tiberias road that I had so often travelled. I thought of the lush and fertile fields, of the hot springs in the Syrian Himmeh, occupied by Israel since 1967, of the beautiful lake. How far it all seemed from here. It was a different world that lay across the river, with another life, another topography, other colours, another history. A land that from here appeared truly like a paradise had been usurped and could not even be visited.

As we left the van someone muttered in a manner expressive of deep-seated frustration about the utter unfairness of the state of the world, 'To think that we are only a half-hour's drive from Tiberias. So near and yet so far.'

*

Ali and Najib agreed to say that Najib was from the village of Tireh, had had a dispute with his people and had come looking for two *dunums* of land on this side of the river.

One of the men who was in on Najib's secret was asked by a newly engaged member of the tribe about the nature of Najib's business here. The man answered that Najib had come to seek a bride. The other man, whose nickname was Azzouz, worried that the sheikh would give his fiancée to Najib, who seemed a better match. So he said, 'I don't believe him. I think he has another purpose in coming here. Have you not noticed how every time he hears someone arriving he gets nervous and looks around him furtively? I feel he is running away from something.'

The first man said that the best way to find out was to take Najib aside and ask him directly, and from the manner of his reply they would know whether he was telling the truth or not.

The two went over to Najib and indicated they wanted to speak to him in private. So the three went to a small hill by the river and sat together. The water rushed past them down the valley as the man who knew Najib's secret said, 'If you've come looking for a bride, then Azzouz is your man. He is an expert on the matter.'

Najib understood the reason for the remark and turned to Azzouz. 'I greatly appreciate your generosity in offering to help me find a bride. God knows I need one. But I have come here for a different purpose. I need to buy two *dunums* and in return I will tend the sheikh's cows. If Azzouz can help me in this matter I will give him his share of the proceeds.'

Azzouz, greatly relieved and comforted, promised to do what he could to help Najib. So he went over to speak to Ali, who told him, 'We are always ready to help a guest. I'll give him the two *dunums* to help him spend his year away from his people, who are bound not to forsake him and will resolve their differences with him eventually. But I will not share my livestock.'

The Arab Revolt in June 1916 against the Ottoman government was led by Hussein Ibn Ali, who had been appointed Emir of Mecca in 1908 by Sultan Abdulhamid, and was supported by the British. It represented their unprecedented response to blunt the force of the Sultan's call to holy war issued at the start of the First World War. But the effect of the British effort at tearing apart the Ottoman Empire from the inside was not immediately evident. It took a few years, extensive efforts by T. E. Lawrence and the distribution of bribe money before hundreds of Arab soldiers and officers began to desert the Ottoman forces and join those of the Sharif of Mecca. The occupation of Aqaba in July 1917 marked a turning point in support for the anti-Ottoman forces. These developments led to panic among Ottoman war leaders. Orders were issued to intensify efforts to clamp down on dissent and to arrest those considered as traitors. It appeared that word had reached the authorities that Najib was in the Jordan Valley, so a detachment of mounted police was sent after him. They knew of the friendship between Najib and Sheikh Mahmoud Tabari, so they directed the force there, hoping to apprehend Najib.

The Ottoman police surrounded Tabari's house. The sheikh went to meet them.

'Why have you come at nightfall?' he queried. 'If you are guests you are welcome. Otherwise tell me what is your purpose in coming here at this hour.'

'We are looking for a friend of yours who is a traitor,' an officer said.

'If I had friends who are traitors I would not conceal them,' retorted Tabari.

'You have a friend whom you favour over your own brother.'

'Yes,' said Tabari, 'I have such a friend, and he is Najib Nassar.'

'He is the man we are looking for.'

'He is not a traitor.'

'It is not our task to determine this. Our mission is confined to searching for the man and capturing him, dead or alive.'

'He is not here.'

'We will search and find the truth.'

'Search as much as you wish.'

The police went around the village asking everyone if they had seen Najib. When they didn't find the man they were looking for, they went to Sheikh Mashouh, the head of the tribe of Sukhor al Ghor, and spent the night with him, letting him know their purpose in coming to the area.

Mashouh did not know the whereabouts of Najib, but to be on the safe side he still sent word to his uncle Ali Shamali across the river, alerting him that the police had come searching for Najib.

Sheikh Ali did not share this bit of news with Najib, in order to avoid causing him further anxiety. He waited until his guests had left, then said, 'As you can see, there are many guests who stop by my house and sometimes they might be police. It is better if you sleep in a different tent every night.' He pointed to a *kharboush* which had been put up in a well-concealed spot and suggested that Najib sleep there.

Ever since seeing this word in Najib's fictional memoir I have wondered what it means. In colloquial Arabic it conveys something haphazard, messy, not done with care. In the course of my visit to Jordan, as we sat on a patio before the garden full of lavender and rosemary bushes, sipping a drink made from rosemary, I asked my host what the word would mean to a Bedouin. I was told it denoted a ramshackle tent pitched any which way and used for storage.

'When did they put this up?' asked Najib.

'Half an hour ago,' Ali replied.

'Then you put it up for me. Is it because you've heard something?'

The sheikh denied having heard anything, claiming he was just being cautious. So Najib crept into the *kharboush*, lay down on the ground and covered himself with his *abba*.

During the night, while Najib slept, the police came, but they did not think of searching the *kharboush*. In the morning Najib woke up refreshed and took a walk along the riverbank until he found a ditch where he could undress and wash unobserved. When he came out the sun had risen and its early-morning rays dried him.

He dressed and covered his face except for his eyes and nose, then climbed a hill behind the wadi and surveyed the beautiful valley with the water running through it. He began to reflect on what would have happened had the proposed land sale gone through. If these good people had been evicted, where would he have taken refuge and what would have become of this lovely valley?

Visiting the same place almost a century later, I recalled Najib's question. The valley has been fragmented by formidable wire fences and mined ground, unreachable, underdeveloped and a source of pain and suffering for its original owners, many of whom cannot use or even visit it any more.

When Najib returned to the village he heard some people say that the officers had searched three villages nearby. Three teams had been simultaneously dispatched to look for him. He was sure that had he been apprehended by these men he would have been treated very roughly and tortured all the way to Nazareth, where he would have been handed over to the authorities. He decided it was time to move again.

*

Towards the end of 1916 T. E. Lawrence, who was fluent in Arabic, was shoring up support for the Arab Revolt and recruiting greater numbers of Arabs to the side of the British in the war. Meanwhile, more intelligence reports than ever were now reaching the authorities, and Najib's name was often mentioned, making it appear that he was a major player behind many plots. News reached him that a homing pigeon had been caught with two messages tied to its legs. These messages were written in English and intended for the British, and Najib, educated at an English school, was suspected of writing them. However, having investigated the matter further, the Ottomans uncovered an espionage ring among the Jewish colonies along the coast and made arrests there. One Jewish woman killed herself before they could get to her for fear that she would be made to confess under torture. Another killed himself in the detention centre in Nazareth. The rest were sent to the military court in Damascus and two of them were hanged. The discovery of this ring created a huge stir and made Ottoman officials and army officers highly suspicious. This made the commander of the army issue strict orders to the *hakim al wilaya* (the provincial governor) to arrest Najib, and the *hakim* in turn sent strict orders to the *mutassarifiyah* (district) of Acre and *qaim makam* (district commissioner) of Haifa to redouble their efforts to find Najib.

This time Najib decided to go to Abdullah al Hussein, the sheikh of the Saqor tribe. (*Saqor*, plural of *saqer*, is Arabic for falcons and it was fitting that the tribe should be so named, because its members moved freely over the hills, unmindful of borders.) To say farewell, Najib did not want to go to see Ali in his tent, because there were always large numbers of guests stopping there, so he suggested meeting at his *kharboush*.

When Ali came Najib told him, 'I believe it has become too dangerous for me to stay with you. I think it is safer for me to go.'

'Where to?' Ali asked.

'To Abdullah al Hussein, Sheikh al Saqor.'

'Abdullah,' said Ali, 'is a generous man, but he likes to stay on good terms with the government. Word has reached me that some notable in Nazareth sent a message to him upon the request of the *qaim makam* of Haifa and has commissioned him to look for you. It is true that a Bedouin would not betray a guest, yet exposing yourself to danger is not advisable.'

'Then I'll go to Emir Bashir al Ghazzawi.'

'Emir Bashir is the emir of us all, but many Nazarenes visit him and they all know you. You should not risk a weak soul mentioning your name to the wrong people.'

'Then I'll go to Taybeh Ibn Alloun in the district of Irbid.'

'And who do you know there?'

'The two sheikhs, Hassan Abdel Wali and Hazaa al Omar.'

'But these days Taybeh is always full of people collecting wood. Many policemen go there, especially to Hassan's house, which is open to guests at all times. Beni Sakher tribesmen have fought with the gendarmerie and killed one or two of them. The government is after them. They come to Taybeh now and then to search the village, hoping to capture them. Your presence there will expose you to danger. I believe it is better for you to stay with us.'

'Let me go and if I get tired I will return. Taybeh is in the *mutassarifiyah* of Hauran, which is part of the *vilayet* of Syria, where I am not known.'

'Then go to the house of Hazaa.'

Ali called one of his men and told him, 'Najib does not like our place and wants to make an arrangement with our neighbours in Taybeh. Prepare two horses and take him there because he does not know the way. Return only after you have arrived safely.'

After leaving the green valley, which was planted with tomatoes, aubergines and cucumbers, we climbed up the hills on the Jordanian side. With lower rainfall than the West Bank, this land is considerably less fertile. There was hardly any terracing on the slopes and little cultivation. The government put a great deal of effort into forestation, but they made the same mistake as Israel, planting Syrian pines, whose acidic leaves destroy the undergrowth. They would have done better to plant native trees, such as the local oak, *Quercus calliprinos*, which survives in arid climates and is protected from grazing animals by a coat of thorns. Although it grows very slowly, its roots can penetrate hard limestone and dolomite.

We drove through rugged terrain with wonderful scenery. As one goes further east the plateau rises and becomes even more uneven. Vast numbers of boulders scattered over the surface become an increasing obstacle to cultivation. The highest part of the plateau is Jabal Druze, an irregular dome of basalt capped by low volcanic cones, the largest of which is Tel Guineh, about 1,500 metres above sea level. Once again Abu Ahmad lost his way and had to find locals to ask for directions.

I was surprised that a driver of a public vehicle would be so constantly in need of directions. Only when we were well into our journey did Abu Ahmad reveal that he was prohibited from driving his taxi outside his designated route, which was to and from the Allenby Bridge and Amman, as was clearly marked on the side of his car. But I had failed to notice it. This, then, was why he grew anxious whenever we passed a checkpoint. He would roll down his window and call out his unusual friendly greeting, '*Marhaba, hukoumeh!*' He was taking a risk by driving me up north.

'They have blockaded us,' he explained, 'by marking our route on the side of the car. Every policeman who now stops me will know I'm off my route. But all they can do is give me a ticket. Thirty dinars. It's a risk I take. It used to be possible for me to go anywhere I wanted. Now I'm under blockade.

'I used to drive cars back from Germany through Europe. I travelled all over – Düsseldorf, Salzburg, Stuttgart, Frankfurt, Cologne, Berne, Lucerne. I picked up a dictionary and would look up words in German and construct sentences. I got to speak enough German to get by. I also used to drive to Istanbul. A driver gets to see places. I've been to more places than my father ever dreamed of visiting. Drivers are like doctors. We examine people and come to know them for what they really are. Quite often they think they will never see me again, that I will never know who they are. We know where they go, how they behave outside their place of residence. We get to know the good ones from the bad. I drive them and listen to their conversations. Especially now that they all have mobile phones, they talk openly, unaware that I'm overhearing.

'I have a brother who makes millions. He's a car dealer. His showroom is in the middle of Amman. He told me, "You are the eldest. Why don't you take a rest from driving? You can come to my shop, just sit and drink coffee and tea, do nothing and take a thousand dinars a month." But I cannot. This work is in my blood. Every day I'm in a different place. If I stop I'll suffer. At my age movement is good. It's important to keep on moving.

'I worked on the route to Iraq until the end of the Iraq–Iran War. I know Baghdad like the palm of my hand, better than I know Amman. Iraq is in my blood. I went all over from Mosul to Basra, Kirkuk, Sulaymaniyah, Arbil, Najaf, Al Kut.

But the best part is the north, where the Kurds live. There are waterfalls so cold that if you put a watermelon under them it would split open. This is how cold the water is. Iraq is a country of many riches: oil, agriculture, cattle. And their women are so beautiful. They had everything. We drove with our lights out during the sorties over Baghdad. More than once I almost got killed. Then I stopped working on that route and began going north to Lebanon, passing through Syria. I worked there during the Lebanese Civil War. Seven times my life came under threat and I was going to die. Once I drove some passengers to Beirut, then waited for fares to go back, but no one wanted to go to Jordan so I decided to return with no passengers. At one of the barricades set up by the Christian Phalange, the avowed enemies of the Palestinians, I was stopped and asked for my nationality. If I said Palestinian I would have been killed right away. They used to kill a man as easily as they would crush a tomato. They wanted to see some identification. If I had shown them my passport they would have discovered I was Palestinian, because it says born in Balata, Nablus. I had to think quickly. I produced my driver's licence. It simply states that I'm Jordanian. I showed it to them. They looked at it and asked me to give my regards to the king of Jordan. "He's a good man, your king," they said. They loved him. I was in a cold sweat when I left them.

'I drove everywhere in Syria. I was not confined to one route like here. I could go anywhere in the country. I visited Halab [Aleppo], Hama, Homs, Tadmor, Tartus, Lattakia. I continued on that route until 2005.'

'Why did you stop?' I asked.

'It was all because of that man, a Palestinian from Yarmuk Refugee Camp. He said he wanted to buy my car and give it to some fellow who was unemployed and he was trying to help. He kept on asking me, "Do you want to sell? Do you want to sell?" One day, it was Ramadan. I was fasting and had stocked my car with all sorts of goods from Syria: apples, cherries, sweets. I didn't want to have passengers. I started on my way home. I got to where the road forked, with one side for those entering Syria and the other for those leaving. Then I saw coming towards me one of those long trailers used for transporting sheep. Its driver had obviously gone to sleep and his vehicle was heading straight for me. On one side of the road was a ditch. I could not go back, so I had only one alternative: to go over the kerb, which fortunately was not high, and into the desert. I escaped. The trailer uprooted six olive trees before it came to a stop. Had I not gone over the kerb I would have been flattened. Nothing would have remained of me or my car. Once I stopped people rushed to me. "It's a miracle that you're alive," they said. One of them cupped his hands round my face. "God must be looking over you," he told me. My windscreen was broken and all along the side of the car the metal was pockmarked from the pebbles that shot at it from the skidding trailer. I found the car still working and drove to the border. There they asked, "What happened to your car?" It took about two thousand dinars to repair. But I paid and got it repaired and continued working on the route. But that man from Yarmuk continued to pursue me, asking, "Do you want to sell? Do you want to sell?" I told him, "Stay off my back." But I knew he had given me the evil eye.

'It's a terrible thing when this happens. If a woman without children sees a woman with a child and gives him the eye, the women returns home and finds that her baby is sick. It happens like this all the time. So one day I was approached by Iraqis. They like me because I speak their dialect. They wanted to go to Jordan. I asked them if they had visas or cards certifying that they were businessmen. I always told them the truth. They said they were OK, so they rode with me and we proceeded to the border. There I saw that man again. He asked me, "Do you want to sell?" This time I said, "If you pay me nineteen thousand dinars, I'll sell." He agreed.

'That afternoon when I drove home I was in a state of delirium, asking myself, "What have I done? What will I do now?" Just after I sold, the fare to Damascus went up from five to ten dinars and the licence for taxis on that route shot up. I could only get another car if I paid twenty-five thousand dinars. I didn't have that much money. For a whole year I stayed at home. I was falling apart. Then someone suggested I work on the bridge route. I decided to do it. Now it's been four years. I've got used to the heat and the flies there. If you try eating a sandwich or smoking a cigarette you constantly have to flail your hands to wave them away. But I'm used to it now.'

I turned to look at Abu Ahmad as he described his downfall, at his hopeful, forced smile, and the thought came to me that had he lived in a land of greater opportunities he would have been among the successful entrepreneurs. He would have charmed his way up through quick, focused steps, taking charge, making things work. I studied his face. It was lined with deep folds etching an optimistic countenance that kept in abeyance the pain and disappointment of the years of constant battling to make it in a world of exploitation and war. The quintessential face of a Palestinian.

Speaking of more optimistic times, Abu Ahmad sang the praises of the Druze. 'I have never encountered more generous people,' he told me. 'If you happen to be visiting at lunchtime it is impossible that they would let you go before you've eaten. They always have a fire going where the coffee continues to be warmed. Their fire never goes out. There is always coffee ready to offer guests.'

This was just like Najib's experience with the Bedouins and their amazing generosity, even at a time of war and widespread hunger and fear. The Druze of Lebanon and Syria with whom Abu Ahmad had been in contact must have been different from their relatives in Israel, among whom I had not experienced this custom.

Until 1948 some of the Bedouin tribes who now live in Jordan moved and owned lands on both sides of the river. Among these were the Ghazzawiyya and the Beni Sakher. But there were pronounced differences in the lifestyles of the Bedouins and the other settled inhabitants of the land. It no longer shows in their style of dress or level of material affluence but in their allegiance to their tribe. They have a deep-bred conviction that though they might venture out into the world for long or short periods, whatever they do and wherever they live they remain part of the collective and their primary allegiance is to their tribe.

During my visit to Taybeh I heard a story about a young man called Azzam, who lived during the time of the British Mandate in what was then known as Transjordan. He had heard of the many opportunities for pleasure in the coastal city of Jaffa and yearned to go, but his father would not allow him to. He kept on praying that his father would die and finally he did. Soon after, Azzam sold his flock, took the money and proceeded to cross the river and travel to Jaffa. There he met some young men and asked them where he could find women to sleep with. They directed him to the police station. Azzam went in and the policemen asked him what he wanted.

'Women to fuck,' he answered.

They stared at him in astonishment.

So he asked, 'What's wrong? I have money and I want women to fuck.'

'Where is your money?' one of them asked. 'Show it to me.'

Azzam emptied his pockets on to the policeman's desk.

The policemen grabbed the money and proceeded to beat Azzam. They then sent him back, his virginity preserved, with torn clothes and no money.

When he returned his friends asked him about his adventure.

'Gather around me,' he said, 'so that I will only have to say it once.'

First he described the city of Jaffa and the sea, which he had seen for the first time. He told them the place was full of wonders that they would not believe existed in this world. Then he said, 'I asked around where I could find women to fuck and they sent me to this place near the sea full of people all dressed up in the same kind of clothes. When I got there one of them began speaking to a man called Hello. I could not see him nor could he see me. I could only hear his voice. This Hello must have been an important man. Everything he told the guys to do they did. They beat me up, just as he ordered, and took all my money. God damn this Hello.'

But these outings were not always so innocent. During the British Mandate Zionist land dealers would invite Bedouin tribesmen to Tel Aviv and exploit their weakness for women to try to con them into selling their land. According to a British report of 1923, two Zionist land dealers, Yisrael Blumenfeld and his partner, Tannenbaum, invited to Tel Aviv the brothers Yusuf and Mutlaq al 'Arsan of the Beni Sakher tribe, which controlled large parts of the Beisan Valley. They took them to bars and brothels. During the night out they then offered a high price for land owned by the tribe. The brothers agreed and sold. However, by 1948, despite a number of sly tactics used by the Zionists to purchase land from the Bedouins,

142

only a small fraction had been sold. Nonetheless, that year the tribes were pushed across the river to the eastern bank, losing all their property to Israel.

In Taybeh Najib was made welcome. It was clear that Hazaa had heard his story. 'I have been very worried about you. Thanks be to God, who led you to us,' he said.

Najib did not need to say anything. Hazaa summoned his eldest son, Matar, and asked him to call his uncle Sheikh Hassan, adding, 'But do not tell anyone that Najib is with us.'

Matar headed for Hassan's house. Whenever he met someone from the village he said, 'Come, let me tell you something.'

When they asked, 'What is it?' he would say, 'Najib Nassar, the fugitive from Jamal Pasha, is here. But don't tell anyone.'

When he arrived at his uncle's house Hassan said, 'Go before me. I will follow later.' And on the way back again everyone Matar met was told the news of Najib's arrival in the village.

By the time he returned to Hazaa's house the place was full of people who had come to greet Najib, because they knew him as the one who had in the past helped Hassan gain acquittal from a false accusation.

Najib asked Hazaa what was happening.

'This Matar cannot keep a secret,' Hazaa answered. 'But do not worry. When Hassan arrives we'll have dinner and after the guests are gone we will discuss what to do.'

Najib ate dinner that night in Hazaa's house with Sheikh Hassan and the village notables, who had come to pay their respects to him. They all drank coffee and talked. Then Najib began to yawn. The guests noticed this and someone said, 'The guest is tired and he should be left alone to rest. Let us leave.'

Najib now sat alone with Hazaa and Hassan and told them the whole story. He finished by saying, 'I have come seeking refuge with you, but now that the whole village knows about me it has become too dangerous to stay with you. Let me hear your suggestions.'

'Some of our men killed two gendarmes and Jamal Pasha issued strict orders that they be pursued. So they fled deep into the wilderness. If you go to them you will be safe from the authorities. We have faithful friends among them and we have good relations with them, so they will regard our guest as their own. They will sacrifice their lives to protect such a guest.'

'No. I don't want to be where I can no longer have news of what is taking place in the country. Also, if I go that far I will be considered a traitor and the government will go after my friends and family because of me.'

'Then do you remember Rushdi?'

'Who is he?'

'Rushdi al Sardi, with whom we share our flock of goats. You helped him when he and I were accused of a crime.'

'Yes, I remember him.'

'You can go and stay with him. He lives secluded in the *heish* [Bedouin slang for tall weeds that do not easily burn in which it is possible to hide].'

'Is it far from here?'

'Not far. Only a two-hour walk away.'

'Does he get many visitors?'

'No, because he is far from the road.'

'Then I will go to him,' Najib agreed, and the three rode together.

From Taybeh Abu Ahmad drove me down to visit Wadi al

Taybeh, the valley through which Najib rode his horse to the *heish*. I was travelling in Jordan during the spring, when the weather is pleasant. But Najib was there in the summer, when it gets unbearably hot.

The land was very hilly and steep, with narrow wadis. The soil here also seemed infertile and there was no terracing anywhere. In the wadi I could see the remains of a flour mill where grain must have been brought to be ground before the flour was transported across the river to be sold in Haifa.

The hill bordering this narrow valley was quite steep. I raced along the path, eager to get a look at the Israeli side. I was so impatient to see the Galilee from this side of the Jordan that I forgot to consider whether I would be able to make it back. On the return journey I had great difficulty negotiating sections of the path. The hill was so steep and the soil so dry, I was worried that if I slipped I would be unable to stop myself from falling right down to the bottom of the wadi. For part of the way I had to crawl on all fours.

There was a spring nearby. This must have been where Najib used to water the goats of the tribesman with whom he was hiding. I could see how this wadi was a continuation of Wadi al Bira, where I had walked not long ago on the other side of the Jordan in the different world of Israel.

With the price of land rising astronomically and tourism taking off in Jordan, dramatic changes are taking place in the lifestyles of many of the Bedouins now settled there. Their images are used in marketing campaigns targeted at European tourists as representing the exotic part of Jordan with their ancient and noble but still living culture. In places such as Petra this often results in bizarre and distressing scenes of alienated young men dressed up and presented in settings that render them an imitation of who they are just for the eyes of the visiting foreign and sometimes local tourists. The disjuncture they surely feel when they return to their natural settings must be difficult to bear.

We stopped at the house of a descendant of a sheikh with whom Najib had stayed. We were served a glass of rosemary water, which we were assured had aphrodisiac qualities. This had become the sheikh's favourite drink. Even though he had some fifteen children, he wanted more. His idol was a neighbour who, with forty children from four wives, did not need to employ strangers on his poultry farm. Our host claimed he knew men who had as many as seventy children. They must drink litres of rosemary water, I thought. When we exhausted the subject of children serving as cheap labour, our host sought my advice on the best stocks to buy. He was asking the wrong man.

Once the horses were readied and Hassan fetched his gun, the three began their night-time ride to the *heish* where Rushdi was camping.

As they approached the camp the dogs began to bark, alerting Rushdi and another sheikh with the apt name of Abu al Kharouf (Father of Sheep). Both went for their guns, calling out, 'Who's there?'

'A friend,' Hassan answered.

'And who have you brought with you?'

'A guest and a dear friend.'

The two tribesmen approached the riders and the women began laying mattresses in the *kharboush*.

'And what brings you so late at night?' Rushdi asked.

Hassan took the man by the arm and walked away with him, whispering into in his ear.

Rushdi returned, took Najib's hand and bent down to kiss it. Najib withdrew his hand as Rushdi proclaimed, 'Thanks be to God, who has blessed this hour and brought you to us so that we can return our debt to you.'

Najib marvelled at the good manners and habits of those living in the wilderness. 'I shall be your guest until God makes it easier on me,' he said.

'As long as I live you are welcome here,' Rushdi answered.

Hassan and Hazaa embarrassed Najib by weeping. Before leaving, Hassan told Rushdi, 'Najib is your charge. Be true to your highest principles and act towards him as befits the best tradition of your people.'

'I don't need to be told this. I will protect Najib as I would protect my own eyes. He is just as valuable.'

The two rode back to return to the village before daybreak, so their absence would remain undetected. They left one horse with Najib in case he should need it.

Najib recounts the last stage of his flight as a romantic episode during which he lived a simple, happy, contented life. This was to be the culmination of the adventure that, in later years, he looked back upon as one of the best periods of his life. It is the only part written with humour. He obviously relished the challenge of having to live so far from any urban centre, totally at one with nature, experiencing as intimately as possible for a non-Bedouin the life of the nomad. While writing, Najib must have been aware that his readers would be urbanites who could never imagine themselves going through an experience like this. He was proving himself the rebel, the renegade from his society, one who believed in living simply and putting his beliefs into practice.

That night Najib slept in the tent with the lambs constantly clambering over him and his thin mattress. He awoke in the morning to find himself in a forest of oak trees, the low native oak Arabs call *ballut*. They were everywhere he looked. Sheep and goats were scattered around the tents of their owners, the women milking them. The morning air was cool and every time a breeze blew the oak leaves were gently ruffled. The children gathered around Najib, examining him, marvelling at his clothes, which were so different from theirs.

When Rushdi awoke he was distressed to find that his guest had risen before him. A host should always get up first, fetch water for the guest to wash his face and hands and then, as the guest lay in his bed, bring him coffee to drink.

Rushdi came over to Najib to invite him to sit and drink coffee. 'Soon,' he said, 'the bread will be baked and we will have breakfast together.'

Najib looked at Rushdi and told him in a determined voice, 'As long as I'm staying with you I don't want to be treated as a guest. I want to be treated like your brother. What I want is to graze your sheep.'

'What? May God forgive me. You, my guest, graze my sheep! You are my master and I will serve you and protect you as I protect one of my own.'

'I know full well how generous you are and what excellent manners you have displayed towards me. But protecting me means that you allow me to graze your sheep. Today you will come with me and teach me how to do it. Tomorrow I will take your youngest son with me and I will guarantee you that your sheep will be well tended,' Najib said firmly. 'Today I will watch how you do it and tomorrow I will go in your stead,' he repeated, leaving Rushdi no choice but to agree.

When the time came, Rushdi got up. He put a few pieces of baked bread in a goatskin bag, took up his staff and, crying, '*Hur hur* [colloquial for make haste, run],' to the sheep, he started walking. The flock responded to his call and began following him. His young son chased the lazy ones, urging them along. Najib meanwhile watched everything carefully.

The procession of sheep, goats, men and the young boy went

into the wilderness, stopping every time they got to a green patch and waiting until the animals had grazed. This routine continued for some three hours, then the flocks were driven down to the gully, where there was a stream that poured into the *ghor* (literally 'low place', in this case the Jordan Valley). As soon as the animals saw the water they trotted to it and drank their fill. Then they moved back into the shade to rest.

Meanwhile Najib had noticed an oleander bush nearby in the middle of the stream. He took off his sandals, waded out and began examining it. Rushdi asked him what it was about the oleander that interested him.

'I have some need for this bush,' Najib replied vaguely, without elaborating. Instead, he leaned against a tree next to Rushdi and watched the herd.

An hour later they had something to eat, then after a little rest Rushdi got up, calling, '*Hur hur, hau hau*,' to the herd, and they started moving in another direction, grazing for another two hours, and finally returned to the camp. And thus ended a day of shepherding.

'I found grazing sheep to be easy but the goats are another matter,' Najib admitted to his host as they were walking back.

'You know,' said Rushdi, 'sheep follow the leader the way we tribal Arabs follow our sheikh. Goats are like you city people. Every one of you is his own man and does as he pleases.'

When they got back the women laid down the mattresses for them to lie on and rest while they lit the fire and made coffee. This pleased Najib, because he loved the bitter Bedouin coffee. But he preferred to lie on the bare ground, finding it cleaner than their mattresses. Rushdi realised he could not argue with Najib and let him do as he wished. Soon an old man about eighty years old joined them and the three drank coffee together.

Najib grew very fond of this old man. Every evening they would spread out their robes on the bare ground and, as they reclined, the old man would tell Najib about the adventures he'd had during his long life. Najib listened very carefully, marvelling at the wonderful manners of the traditional tribesmen, behaviour he yearned to find among his own townsmen. The more he came to know the habits of the people he was now living among, the more he dreamed of that time when people led lives of happy simplicity away from urban centres, the ambitions they breed and the corruption and wickedness of the city-dwellers.

Once a week Hazaa and Hassan would come to visit and check that Najib was doing well. They found him happy and contented with his new surroundings and his life among these generous tribesmen.

As I read Najib's account, written during the British Mandate, of the time he spent in the wilderness with the Bedouins, a period he insists on describing as unconditionally happy and fulfilling, I wondered how much of this had to do with how depressed he was when he was writing it. His health was failing and he was suffering from a strong sense of disillusionment and betrayal as he observed the more affluent members of the middle class around him preoccupy themselves with emulating the British, whom they regarded as culturally superior, in superficialities like dress and outward behaviour, rather than pursuing the struggle for liberation to which he was so ardently devoted. In an article he wrote in 1922 he laments how, with the arrival of the British with their trappings of modernity, owners of large expanses of agricultural land were charmed and proceeded to emulate the external appearance of the British, trying to eat and dress like them and also to drink spirits like them, rather than trying to learn from them how to modernise their agriculture. Soon their expenditure exceeded their income and they were forced to sell their land cheap, so becoming strangers in their own country.

Such was now Najib's routine. Every day he took out the sheep and goats to graze, while Rushdi used the free time thus afforded him to dress up and go to the village to visit with friends. One day Najib borrowed soap from Rushdi and, while the herd was drinking, went to the oleander bush he had spotted on that first excursion, took off his clothes, washed them in the water and spread them out to dry while he washed himself. This was how he was able to keep clean after sharing a tent with the animals.

This idyllic life lasted for twenty-six days, during which, Najib says, he felt perfectly happy and content except for two things: worrying about the fate of friends who had helped him and the lice that he felt were devouring him alive.

He was too far away for news of his friends to reach him, but he could, perhaps, do something about the lice.

'You have plenty of fresh air and lots of sunshine and there are ropes placed for hanging things,' he said to Rushdi. 'Why don't you tell the women to hang up the clothes to get them aired and sunned?'

'What for?' Rushdi asked.

'To get rid of the lice.'

'Lice don't come from the clothes.'

'Where, then, do they come from?'

'Lice come from your skin.'

Najib smiled to himself but did not try to convince his host otherwise. He knew it would be futile.

The following morning Najib told Rushdi he was feeling tired. The noon sun was much too hot. It baked the land and made it difficult for him to breathe. He said he would like to get some rest and asked to be excused from grazing for the day.

'You go,' he told Rushdi, 'and let me sleep in the shade of that oak tree.'

Rushdi took the flock while Najib went into the copse and found a big tree. He wrapped himself in his *abba* and slept, feeling the soft warm breeze moving through his long beard. After two hours he woke up and thought he would try to get rid of the infernal lice. So he climbed the tree and found two parallel branches to sit on, took off his clothes, hung them out and began examining them for lice.

As Najib sat in the tree picking out lice and tossing them away, he began to ask himself how he had ended up like this, grazing sheep, living and sleeping in their pen. His brother Ibrahim and his wife, Katbeh, came to mind. Together they ran the Nassar Hotel in Haifa, which was renowned for its cleanliness and superb fare. And here he was, picking lice from his clothes. What would they think if they saw him now?

I had an intimation of what they might have thought from the often repeated description that my grandmother Julia, Najib's niece, gave of her uncle when he arrived at the hotel bearded, thin and, as she emphasised, 'smelling terrible'.

But Najib brushed the thought aside. It did not really matter what they thought. He was enjoying this life and would not change it for any other. In fact he would not mind continuing like this, abandoning urban life altogether. He was amazed how, with the wilderness all around him, he felt he was living on an island surrounded by a different sea. He had never felt so close to nature, such oneness with it. By day he was entering deeper into the life of the wilderness, thinking only about sheep and goats and that old man and their nocturnal talks under the open sky. This was the only time in his life that he lived so far away that he had no news of the war or of his children or brothers. He was totally self-absorbed and utterly content. It was as though he had shrugged off the cares of the world, all those concerns that had never left him throughout his previous life and he had never imagined could be cast off. Now he could see that it was possible. He was able to shed them as easily as he shed his clothes. They had been a constant source of irritation, just like these lice. And they could be got rid of merely by tearing them away and letting the sun and water do the cleansing.

Najib was absorbed in his clothes, his body and his thoughts when the silence was broken by the sound of horses approaching. Assuming this was the gendarmerie coming to get him, he moved to one side to completely conceal himself, while keeping watch through the branches of the tree. When the horses got closer he was able to recognise Hazaa and Hassan, so he quickly got dressed and waited. Then he saw a young man whom he thought was one of Rushdi's boys coming towards him and waving. He felt certain that the police had come to get him. What he had was too good to last, a luxury he couldn't afford for long. That other world to which he had once belonged, that world of obligations and family, of middle-class concerns and values that he had succeeded in abandoning, had crossed the wilderness to intrude on the island of tranquillity where he had found refuge. Accompanied by the young man, whom he now recognised as his nephew, he walked from the tree to the men.

When he approached he saw that both Hassan and Hazaa were armed and were accompanied by two other young men.

After Najib had greeted his visitors, Hassan said, 'Our guests came to us asking to see you, but we denied that we knew your whereabouts. Because of his fair skin we suspected that your nephew was a German officer. He said he had been directed by Sheikh Ali to come to us. We knew that the sheikh never lies and that you had indeed passed by Taybeh. Still we didn't reveal your whereabouts. Then we made your nephew swear on the Bible that he is indeed who he says he is. Only then did we agree to bring them here. But, as you see, we have come armed, so that if we see any sign that they mean you harm we will kill all of them and whisk you away.'

Najib was pleased to hear how concerned they were that no harm should befall a guest and he thanked them for their caution. But he still felt disoriented. He was being forced to deal once again with the world of politics, family obligations and friends whom he was putting in danger. Once again he thought about surrender. He would be subjecting himself to grave danger, yet decide he must. First, though, he would allow himself time. He would listen fully to what his nephew had to say. This would help him to recover his former way of speaking and to revive the old concerns that he had managed to lose as he spent time isolated from his society, living like a true nomad with the Bedouins.

He stood up, gesturing to his nephew, Hassan, Hazaa and the two other young men to follow him. When they were all seated in the shade of a tree Najib turned to his nephew. 'Now tell me what news you carry with you.'

After the young man had answered all of Najib's enquiries about his cousins, his children and his brothers, he began to tell Najib about the searches that had taken place in all the houses of their relatives, and how orders would periodically come to conduct more.

'The authorities laid siege to all the places where you had taken refuge, one neighbourhood after another. Then they sent horsemen in different directions to pursue you. We lived in constant fear that they would find you and hang you. Then a bounty of fifty riyals was placed on your head. When this failed to bring results, the *mutassarif* of Acre came to see us in Nazareth. He was accompanied by Fawzi Bey Malaki. He told us that an order had come from the head of the army to arrest Abdullah Mukhlis, Kamel Kawar, Issa al Douri and your brother Rashid and send them to the military tribunal in Damascus unless they informed the authorities of your whereabouts. Each one of them was summoned separately and told of this order. Abdullah Mukhlis was still of the opinion that you should not give yourself up. He sent word urging us, if we knew your whereabouts, to warn you against giving yourself to death and to advise you to stay in hiding and keep as far away as possible, and to reassure you that nothing will happen to your brother and your friends at the military court, whereas if you surrendered you would be in mortal danger. But he has been dropped from the list to be arrested if you're not found because he was able to convince the authorities that he did not know of your whereabouts. As to Kamel Kawar, Issa Douri and my uncle, they thought otherwise. They said they were persuaded by the assurances they got from Fawzi Bey and the *mutassarif* that you will not be hanged and that it was better that you should surrender and release yourself from your misery and release them from their responsibility.

'It happened that Jamal Pasha Junior was passing through Nazareth and heard of the latest developments in your case, so he summoned Fadel Fahhoum to him. "They tell me you're a friend of Najib's," he began. Fadel admitted that he was. "Then take my advice and tell him to give himself up."

'"Believe me, Pasha," Fadel insisted, "I do not know his whereabouts. But should I learn where he is I will relay your message."

'"Go look for him and convince him to give himself up immediately," repeated the Pasha.

'But Fadel was unable to elicit a promise from Jamal Pasha regarding your safety, and this is why he does not advise that you give yourself up. But he says if you do he would be willing to accompany you to the military court.

'As for my father and Kamel, they instructed me to find you and inform you of what is taking place. They stressed that I should leave it to you to decide, but you should do so in a manner that would not lead you to blame yourself should anything happen to any one of your friends.'

Najib asked, 'And has anyone accused me of anything since the incident with the homing pigeon?'

He was told that his name had been mentioned when they found the pigeon with the messages, but after they uncovered the espionage ring people realised they were wrong to suspect him.

Najib now looked at the men around him. 'If anyone has an opinion let me hear it. It is difficult for me to make up my mind.'

Hassan said, 'I believe you should go deeper into the wilderness and let the house bewail him who built it.'

Next it was Hazaa's turn to speak. He said, 'I am also of Hassan's opinion. Nothing will happen to those of your friends who might be taken to the military court. But in your case the rope with which you would be hanged would be closer to you than the collar of your shirt if you should decide to give yourself up.'

Najib felt he had heard enough. 'You are all witnesses to what I'm going to say. I know that Hassan and Hazaa would prefer that I not give myself up. As I am their guest, they are willing to do whatever it takes to get me as far away from the area of jurisdiction of Jamal Pasha as possible.'

'What you say is true,' Hassan said. 'Just say now that you want to escape. We have our horses and our weapons. We'll take you wherever you want to go.'

Najib continued, 'I'm well aware that the assurances of the *mutassarif* are worth nothing. He was instructed to arrest me. Once he does, his mission ends. All he can do is write a word on my behalf which might or might not have any effect. All he wants is to gain favour at my expense. As to Fawzi Bey Malaki, he has been sacked as *qaim makam* and has gone to serve the *mutassarif* in the hope that his good report will get him reappointed. Perhaps he also wants the reward of fifty golden riyals. If it were only my brother who was threatened with being taken to the military court, then I would have found solace in thinking that whatever he suffers because of me he is after all my brother. But should any harm come to the friends who treated me so well in my time of need, should any of them be taken to the military court and be harmed, then I would feel unbearable pain the rest of my life. This is why I have decided to give myself up and suffer the consequences.'

When Najib said this Hassan's head dropped. Hazaa lifted his to the heavens. His nephew froze in place. For a minute the thought of his children crossed Najib's mind and made him silent.

Hassan and Hazaa made their way to the camp. They found Rushdi and told him that Najib had decided to give himself up. Rushdi's expression turned solemn but he said nothing. After a short while food was brought. They all ate with Najib, who was putting on a brave face and pretending for the sake of his friends and companions that he was unconcerned about what was to come. They too were trying to express optimism to reassure him, but neither attempt was successful and the men ate in silence, their grave faces betraying the worry which filled their hearts and minds.

After coffee was brought and drunk, Najib asked for the horses. He held Rushdi's hand, gripping it firmly as he thanked him for his hospitality and care. Then he went to Abu

Kharouf; who was so moved that he took the tip of his *abba* and wiped a tear from his cheek. When Najib said, 'Let us ride,' each mounted the horse that had been readied for him.

Hassan proposed that they ride to Taybeh, saying, 'You can stop there, eat dinner and then leave at night in God's care.'

Najib accepted this suggestion. He wished to avoid meeting any soldiers, so preferred not to ride in broad daylight.

After midnight Najib rode forth from Taybeh with his nephew and his two friends, reaching the Jordan Valley by dawn. They stopped at the house of Mashouh al Labbon, the sheikh of Sukhor al Ghor. He made them have breakfast with him and rest awhile. Then they rode on again and when they were at some distance from their destination Najib asked his three companions to go before him to the house of Sheikh Ali Shamali.

'Tell him that I have decided to give myself up. Eat lunch with him and then return by evening to Wadi al Bira, where you'll find me in a cave with my horse outside it.'

Najib's nephew asked his uncle why they shouldn't continue on to Nazareth.

Najib said that he was worried about encountering the gendarmerie, explaining, 'They would accompany us to Nazareth and claim that they arrested me. Any advantage to be gained from giving myself up would then be lost.'

The nephew and the two others proceeded to Shamali's campsite while Najib rode on to Wadi al Bira, left the road, tethered his horse and left it to graze, then found a stone, rested his head on it and, wrapping himself in his *abba*, tried to get some sleep. He was utterly exhausted.

Everything had happened too quickly for him to adapt to his new circumstances and he wanted to spend some time alone. He needed to think in solitude and be perfectly sure he was willing and able to return. He slept peacefully and was awakened by a voice calling out his name: 'Najib, Najib.'

Half asleep, he asked himself whether he was already back. Was this the voice of authority? No, it was still a voice from the free world he had briefly sampled.

'Come with me,' it said. 'You can still choose freedom over slavery.'

'Should I go?' Najib wondered.

He followed the horseman with his eyes and wept for what he was about to lose for ever.

7

A'yn Anoub

The intricacies of visa regulations made it impossible for me to travel from Jordan, where Najib had taken refuge, to Damascus, where he was later brought to appear before a military tribunal. But I could make it to Lebanon, where I wanted to visit the village of A'yn Anoub in the Lebanese mountains where Najib was born and spent his early years. So Penny and I decided to fly to Beirut. When we arrived at Amman Airport we found that our seats had been given to other passengers. It was such an ordeal to get on the flight that we began to wonder whether this trip was worth taking. But when we woke up the next morning to a gloriously clear and sunny winter's day in Beirut and contemplated the lovely view of the blue Mediterranean from our hotel window, we felt differently.

The beautifully laid-out breakfast buffet also reminded me why Lebanon has that special place in my heart, proof that whoever said the way to an Arab man's heart is through his stomach was right. There was not one but five kinds of white cheese. The sliced tomatoes were surrounded by young sprigs of spring onion and sprinkled with fresh mint so fragrant one could smell it from a distance. We piled our plates with these delicacies and took them to our table. The first mouthful brought back memories of similar food I used to enjoy at my grandmother Julia's table. We ate slowly, savouring every morsel and trying to work out how to replicate these exquisite flavours in our own kitchen. We ultimately decided to grant that the allure of Lebanon is in its food, then leave it at that.

On the way to A'yn Anoub, on a mountain road, we stopped at a pharmacy in a village to get Penny some cold medicine. As I bought the aspirin, I asked about A'yn Anoub and whether there were any members of the Nassar family still left in the area.

'Yes, there are,' the pharmacist told me. 'There is Fahd Nassar.'

'How can we find him?'

'Easy. Just ask at the butcher's. When you get to A'yn Anoub, go to the butcher, you can't miss his shop, and ask him where Fahd is.'

I don't remember ever having visited the village, though my sister Siham, who has an excellent memory, insists that we all have. She even described the house we went to, which she said had a long porch with a balustrade. As we drove through the Lebanese mountain villages, including Souk al Gharb, which I was sure I had visited more than once, I realised how much of Lebanon and our annual summer visits there I had blocked out of my conscious memory. Until 1967, when Israel occupied the West Bank, we used to make the arduous drive to Lebanon, passing through Syrian and Lebanese borders, where my father was often stopped and questioned. My relationship with the place was never simple. The two years I spent at the American University of Beirut from 1971 to 1973, just before the civil war began in 1975, were happy ones. Yet on my last day in the city I found myself brimming with anger. Nothing happened that I had not experienced previously, yet it all seemed unbearable. The taxi driver wanted to add an extra charge and my landlady made unreasonable demands. It was as though the city was determined to send me off angry. I do not lose my temper easily, but that day I felt the need to do something that I had never done before and have never since repeated. I took a bottle of the locally produced Almaza beer and smashed it in the sink. The image of the kitchen sink spattered with green-tinted glass splinters and the severed bottle neck remained with me for many years, a symbol, perhaps, of this city of contrasts and my mixed feelings towards it.

In the summer of 1958, when I was six years old, I came to Beirut with my mother and grandmother to be with my father, who was exiled from Jordan for his political opposition to the regime. We stayed at a modest family hotel near the lighthouse. We were short of money. The place had no air conditioning and I was not used to that degree of heat and humidity. I was so miserable that I went on hunger strike. My parents decided to send me back to Ramallah with my grandmother. I hated the city and refused to look from the window of the plane as we were leaving, or to say goodbye. Instead I cursed it, using the strongest language of which I was then capable, *Tuz* (my arse).

Years later my childish invective developed into serious vilification of the city and its people. When I was in London in 1975, pursuing my law degree, I would read reports in the daily papers about the bloody violence of the civil war that was destroying Lebanon. One particular image stayed with me. It was at the Karantina (now featuring a large concert hall and dotted with art galleries), where the Lebanese right-wing Phalangist fighters committed a gruesome massacre of Palestinians. With corpses strewn on the ground, a group of young hippie-looking Lebanese men wearing large, wide-brimmed hats stood by, playing their guitars. Perhaps this image affected me so deeply because when I was an adolescent in the small town of Ramallah I had held up the young Lebanese as models of sophisticated cosmopolitan youth. The land which I had once regarded as full of promise, culture and taste had proven a prodigious disappointment. The people I had looked up to and admired had turned into perpetrators of horrific murders against my compatriots. I had failed to appreciate that civil wars bring out the worst in people and can turn them into monsters. This was only among the first of many massacres that were to follow in which all sides, including the Palestinians, were implicated.

How could I go back to Lebanon as a tourist, I argued with myself, seeking pleasure in a place where there was so much gratuitous violence? I might go into a restaurant to enjoy one of those fabulous Lebanese meals and, unawares, sit next to a killer, exchanging pleasantries with him as though nothing had ever happened. Any waiter or taxi driver might be one of them. I decided to stay away and so did not return for thirty-five years. But then, with the violence in the Middle East, at home and abroad, I thought that if I continued to avoid all conflict-ridden countries, there would be very few places left for me to visit. I live in a violent region of the world and I had better get used to it. Two years ago I changed my mind and returned to the city that had made its mark on me. Then, the summer after my return, the Israeli army invaded, killed thousands of people, laid waste the country's infrastructure and destroyed a part of the capital, as well as the beautiful villages in the south. I had made my peace with the city too soon.

The city that had had a sweet fragrance now reeked of car fumes and cigarettes. Its inhabitants no longer seemed charming and glamorous. They had a worried downtrodden look. In the face of the many disasters that had befallen them, the Lebanese had proven resilient and capable of weathering the civil war and the many invasions by Israel. This time round though they seemed to be salvaging the private and personal at the expense of the shared and public, destroying many of the city's once attractive neighbourhoods and unique countryside.

With the negligible number of tourists visiting the country because of the Israeli incursions that preceded the outright invasion, and the mysterious explosions that continued to rock the capital, killing major political figures along with whoever was unfortunate enough to be around, the Lebanese economy was suffering. I felt rich and, with money to spend, welcome. I was reminded of what my father used to tell me about his visits from Palestine before 1948. He would be greeted with smiling faces and great attentiveness because Palestinians were known to be good spenders with money to spare. However, the 1948 Nakba impoverished my father, along with so many others, and though he managed to get back on his feet, when he visited Beirut he was no longer the lavish spender he used to be. We had returned to being villagers visiting the big city, poor relatives who required so much and who tried their hosts' patience and strained their resources. The tables have turned again. All my rich relatives having fled Lebanon during the civil war three decades earlier, I was now visiting my poorest relation in A'yn Anoub who could not afford to leave and had stayed behind.

With four children in tow, staying at a hotel for two weeks, eating out and shopping, our annual summer trips must have cost my parents a fortune. Our Nassar relatives were either struggling or had only recently made some money. In both cases they did not want to be burdened with hosting a large family like ours. Our visits could not have been very welcome, especially because my family was seriously judgemental. There was constant grumbling about unmet requests arising from unreasonable expectations more suited to the smaller town of Ramallah than to a metropolitan city like Beirut. Here they lived in small flats and often struggled to make ends meet. My grandmother Julia had an axe to grind with her brothers, blaming them for not taking good care of their mother, Katbeh, when she was alive. I was too young to make up my own mind and the time we spent in Lebanon was always too short to really get to know my Lebanese relatives. I had managed to wipe all recollection of these visits from my mind, exercising that useful talent for selective memory that I inherited from my mother, an acknowledged expert at the practice.

By the 1970s the influx of money from oil-rich Arab countries gave the city the opportunity to play host to spectacularly wealthy Gulf Arabs with whom we could not possibly compete. Beirut became their playground, with a casino, a thriving prostitution industry and an abundant legal supply of alcohol: a Christian city in the Arab world where what was prohibited by Islam could be enjoyed openly without the need to travel to the West – not unlike the role Christian Ramallah is now playing in Palestine. It was also the city with the best universities in the Arab world and the largest publishing houses, which could publish more freely than those in any of the surrounding police states. So there was a flourishing cultural life, with writers, artists and intellectuals; university life as well as a life of abandon, with fine dining, gambling and prostitution. There was the sea for swimming in summer and the snowy mountain slopes for skiing in winter, with picturesque mountain villages providing excellent resorts and escape in the summer from Beirut's oppressive heat and humidity.

As I approached the Nassar family village, I thought of how our two Christian families, now living so far apart, the Shehadehs in Ramallah in the central hills of Palestine and the Nassars in A'yn Anoub in the Lebanese mountains, had been brought together. The Christians of Palestine are the only indigenous Christian community in the world. They and the other Arab Christians in the eastern Mediterranean began as members of the Greek Orthodox Church, known in Arabic as Al Rum al Orthodox, in reference to the Eastern Roman or Byzantine Empire, with its centre in Constantinople.

At the beginning of the last century Najib was involved in the centuries-long struggle of Arab Orthodox Christians to win back control over their church. For the past four centuries successive Greek patriarchs in Jerusalem had been exercising sole power in the patriarchate, making the unfounded claim that they were the direct heirs of everything Byzantine and so all the buildings erected by Constantine and his mother, Helena, in Jerusalem, including the Church of the Holy Sepulchre, belonged to the Greeks. The church in Jerusalem was dealt with as a piece of valuable property owned by a foreign country. For centuries only Greek nationals have been permitted to join the Brotherhood of the Holy Sepulchre, from which the top leadership of the church is chosen.

The patriarchate in Jerusalem owns many valuable properties in Jerusalem and elsewhere in Palestine and Israel, donated over the years to the patriarchate by its Arab members. Many of these have been sold to Israeli institutions and Jewish settlers. The disaffection between the local congregation and the church leadership contributed to the attrition of the Orthodox congregation, as more Arab Christians joined the Western churches, Catholic and Protestant, that were being established in Palestine. The irony is that the fate of my family and their release from the Orthodox sway came through an Anglican mission that was initially sent to the Holy Land to convert Jews to Christianity. After they had succeeded in converting only a tiny number of Jews, they turned their proselytising attention to the Arab Christians and began luring members of the Orthodox faith to the Protestant faith.

The Protestants met with success at almost exactly the same time in the last quarter of the nineteenth century in two remote areas of the Middle East, Ramallah and A'yn Anoub, convincing two heads of families to take the bold step of leaving the church to which their families had belonged for centuries and joining the Protestant Church. Both men had the same first name, Jirius (which is spelt Jirjis in Lebanon); the Nassar Jirius had even served as a cleric of the Orthodox Church. Perhaps they joined the Protestant denomination with an eye to the benefits that such a move promised, perhaps from conviction that the church doctrine being preached was more convincing or perhaps simply because they were fed up with the Greek control of their church. Whatever the reasons, the two families were instrumental in the establishment of a Protestant presence in their respective villages. In Lebanon the Presbyterians went on to establish hospitals and schools, some of which later developed into outstanding universities, such as the American University of Beirut.

In the nineteenth and early twentieth centuries Arab Christians constituted around 11 per cent of the Arab population of Palestine, but with the exception of Lebanon they have never held political power or expressed the desire to translate their religious identity into a political one.

The *millet* system instituted by the Ottomans was the

first attempt at creating out of the diverse members of one sect a singular group. But not one with national rights. Each *millet* had control over matters of personal status, including marriages, inheritance and other religious affairs. This system has outlived the Ottoman Empire. To a large extent it is still followed in the Arab countries of the Levant, as well as in Israel. The government of the British Mandate in Palestine, which took over from the Ottomans after the Allied victory in the First World War, continued it, as did the governments of Jordan, Israel and the Palestinian Authority. But the Mandate government did more than recognise the Jewish population in Palestine as a separate *millet*; the terms of the Mandate endorsed the Zionist belief that Jews constituted a nation entitled to self-determination and thus facilitated the creation in Palestine of a Jewish home which eventually succeeded in taking over the whole of Palestine from the Palestinian Arabs, whether Christian, Jewish or Muslim.

As we drove through some of these villages I tried to revive memories of previous visits, but little was coming back. As the pharmacist had advised, when we got to A'yn Anoub we stopped at the butcher's. He was dressed in the typical clothes of Lebanese mountain men: baggy black trousers and long white jacket that gave the impression of solidity and rooted-ness. He also had the typical thick bushy moustache. When we asked about Fahd Nassar he answered, with a twinkle in his eye, 'You're looking for Fahd Nassar? I'll tell you where you can find him. You see that shop up those stairs? That's where he'll be.'

I climbed, full of excitement and anticipation. Penny followed, sniffling and sneezing. In a blacksmith's shop I found Hani, a young man in his twenties who resembled anything but a scruffy blacksmith. He was close-shaven, fair-skinned and handsome. He wiped his hands before shaking mine. His clean appearance made him look like someone more suited to an office than a metal workshop.

'You're looking for my father? He's at home. I'll take you to him.'

As we walked together I tried to recall the only picture I had seen of Najib. As a younger man would he have looked like a larger version of Hani? Perhaps, but the expression in his eyes would have been different. Hani's expression was carefree and slightly ironic. Had the move to Palestine robbed Najib of that devil-may-care attitude to life one sees so much of around here, or was he disposed towards seriousness irrespective of where he lived? From everything I had read and heard about him, he seemed like a forthright man of principle. In the photograph I have of him, pen in hand, he has a dogged expression that suggests absolute focus and determination.

Penny and I walked into a room constructed over an old building. Inside we saw Fahd sitting in an armchair in front of a wooden stove.

'My father,' Hani announced, theatrically stretching both arms in his direction.

Fahd was not much taller than me, with an unshaven face but kind, enquiring eyes. His thick rough hand shook mine. So much can be determined by the touch of a hand. The shape is always revealing, but only the touch will tell you how soft or hard the skin is, and what sort of life its owner has led. There was warmth in Fahd's handshake. He was welcoming, though somewhat embarrassed about the condition of his room. It had the comforting smell of firewood.

I tried to understand what it was. A sitting room? A kitchen? An all-purpose room? There were a few chairs around the stove, a sink and a fridge, but no bed. It looked like a place where someone might spend the day but sleep elsewhere.

On a side table he had fruit: clementines and bananas, the delicious small Lebanese ones. He offered us some.

'From my trees,' he said. 'They're very good. Please have one. Let me offer you some coffee.'

We declined. 'We don't want to trouble you,' I said.

'It's no trouble at all. It's already made.'

He began to apologise for the place: 'It's still unfinished. I'm working on it.'

I looked around. I could not understand how this room would fit with the rest of the structure through which we had passed.

'Our coffee is strong,' Fahd began explaining to Penny, assuming we lived in America. 'You are used to Nescafé. This is different.'

I looked at Penny, who only said she liked Arabic coffee. She didn't say we always make it, nor did I, even when I realised he thought we were the ubiquitous relatives from America. I was enjoying the explanations that one usually hears a Middle Easterner give to a Westerner when attempting to elucidate our culture and way of life. Among village people this is often accompanied by claims that men from the Middle East are more virile and therefore used to stronger tastes and a harsher way of life than Western men, who have been softened by the affluent, easy lives they lead.

Now that we were settled, Fahd asked, 'Tell me who you are and what brings you here.'

'I am Raja,' I said. 'Julia Nassar's grandson. Do you know Julia?'

He showed no sign of recognition.

'Julia is the daughter of Ibrahim Nassar, who left A'yn Anoub in 1890 and went to Haifa.'

'Yes, I know we had uncles who went to Palestine.'

'Perhaps you've heard of Najib Nassar?' I asked Hani.

'No,' he said.

'Pity,' I said. 'Najib was a great man. You'll find him mentioned in the history books. He was the first Arab to write about Zionism and warn against the Zionist project in Palestine.'

'I never heard of him.'

'You are a Nassar?' Fahd asked.

'No, I'm a Shehadeh. We are originally from Ramallah. My grandfather Salim studied in the United States. Like the Nassars of Haifa, he was a Protestant. When he wanted to get married he was told there was a beautiful woman in Haifa from a Protestant family.'

I looked around the room. Everyone was listening attentively.

'He went to Haifa and enquired about her. He was told he would find her in the church. So he went there and saw Julia Nassar, the daughter of Ibrahim, your relative, playing the organ. She looked beautiful. She also had a strong personality and Salim immediately fell in love with her. They married and lived in Jaffa. Their daughter Wedad is my mother. She and my father also lived in Jaffa. But in 1948 all of them were forced to leave. Salim went to Beirut, where he died soon afterwards. Julia and my parents settled in Ramallah. My grandmother always said her father had come from A'yn Anoub. It was the place I always heard about as I was growing up. This is my first visit. Are there other Nassars left in the village?'

'I and my family are the only ones.'

'Do any of them ever come to visit?'

'For a while they kept up their houses. There was one woman who came in the summer. I'll show you her place. The family owned quite a bit of property in this area.'

'Can we look around?'

'Of course,' he said, standing up.

We climbed the stairs.

'Do you want to see the beautiful view from the roof?' Fahd asked.

'I'd love to,' I replied.

The scenic bay of Beirut stretched below us. A'yn Anoub is only twenty-two kilometres from Beirut and sits atop a steep incline, commanding a beautiful vista of the city and the sea. Closer to the house I could see the medium-sized village spreading out below.

The street where we had parked the car seemed to be a main artery. Below it was a wooded area with two hillocks, like the humps of a camel. The hills were uninhabited. The village meandered through the elevated ground below us. Clearly there was a lot of vacant land, left by its owners to which they never returned.

'What a beautiful view of Beirut you have from here.'

When the Israelis invaded we could see the exploding shells at night,' Fahd told us. 'Just like a great display of fireworks.'

'Were you frightened?'

'Not at all. We came up here to watch. It was a gorgeous sight,' said Hani with a mischievous smile.

I didn't know what to say. I could only think of myself watching the bombing on my small television screen with a sinking heart, thinking that if Israel could do this to the metropolis of Beirut with the whole world watching and no international outcry, what would they do to us in Ramallah when they got the chance?

The view of Beirut from here, with its perfect bay, reminded me of Haifa, further to the south. The similarity must have helped Najib feel at home there. But the migration of Najib and his brothers to Palestine happened very long ago and there seemed to be no stories of their journey. The last quarter of the nineteenth century was a time of turmoil and famine in the Lebanese mountain villages. There was a lot of fighting between the Maronite and Druze communities. Many Christian villages were attacked and a large number of people killed. Could Najib and his brothers have been fleeing the sectarian fighting? Or was it the bad economic conditions that drove them away? In 1890 it was possible for Najib to travel from his village in the Lebanese mountains to Haifa without crossing any borders. Both belonged to the same province, the *vilayet* of Beirut. A hundred years ago the present division of the eastern Mediterranean into Turkey, Lebanon, Syria, Jordan, Israel and Palestine did not exist. The whole region was part of the Ottoman Empire and had been since it was conquered in 1445.

To the north of A'yn Anoub lies the village of Shimlan, a very early centre of Protestantism in the area. Najib's father, Jirjis, was a *khoury*, a Greek Orthodox priest. When I asked Sauheil, Ibrahim's great-grandson, who now lives in London, why he thought the family left A'yn Anoub, he said he had heard that Father Jirjis had been influenced by the Presbyterians and had tried to apply some of their creeds in his church. For this he was reprimanded by the bishop and told he was violating Orthodox beliefs. He then became fed up with the old rituals and fossilised mentality and turned Protestant.

There was much to gain from making that conversion. The Syrian Protestant College (later the American University of Beirut, where I studied) had already been established and Protestants could get a free university education there. When I checked the archives of the university I found that a good number of Nassars had graduated from it, mostly in pharmacy. Sauheil also thought that Ibrahim must have heard that there were good schools in Palestine, established by the Protestant missionaries, where he would be able to enrol his children. I don't know whether education was the primary incentive. I found neither Ibrahim's nor Najib's name among the graduates of the American University, though I did find the name of their brother Rashid, who graduated as a pharmacist. The record said that he worked as a pharmacist in Safad. Could he have been the first of the brothers to go to Palestine, from where he wrote back to encourage the others to follow?

At the university library I was relieved to find a microfiche copy of *Al Karmil*, Najib's newspaper. It bore the imprimatur of the Hebrew University of Jerusalem. Many years ago in Beirut Sauheil had asked the regional director of the Collège des Frères to buy a copy for him during one of the director's work trips to Jerusalem, where Sauheil could not go. I had been dreading the prospect of having to find a way to get permission to enter the fortress-like Hebrew University to read it there. With his booming voice and dry humour, so characteristic of the Nassar men, Sauheil told me, 'The Israelis took everything – our country, even our home libraries. It is good we were able to escape with the clothes on our backs.'

Until I found out that Rashid had graduated as a pharmacist from the American University of Beirut I had been trying to imagine how a family from a small, relatively poor Lebanese mountain village that had suffered civil strife for years could have ventured into a strange land where they knew no one. How did they manage? How could they have started their hotel business with their scant resources? But now I knew that one of the brothers was working as a pharmacist at a Protestant hospice in Palestine, I understood how Najib had a place where he could start a new life. I had always known that my grandmother Julia and her sister Hanna were born in Tiberias. Najib worked at the Scottish Hospice in Tiberias. The family was proficient in English, thanks to the Protestant School in Souk al Gharb, not far from A'yn Anoub. Najib was given an administrative job. Katbeh, Ibrahim's wife and my great-grandmother, with her culinary skills, must have helped in the kitchen, or might even have run it for the hospice.

After working for a few years and saving some money, they must have decided to try their luck further west in Haifa, a growing port city with many itinerant merchants and missionary visitors but no guest house. This might have given them the idea of starting a small hostel with a restaurant where travellers could be served the excellent Lebanese fare prepared by Katbeh.

The only family portrait that survives, which my grandmother always displayed on the table in the vestibule of her home in Ramallah, shows Katbeh, a woman with an attractive face, sitting on the edge of her chair with both feet firmly on the ground and hands on the armrests, ready to leap up and go back to her kitchen as soon as the photograph was taken. She looks sturdy, industrious and down to earth. She is wearing a dark *toub* (traditional dress) rather than trying to look Western, like many of her peers at the time. Her husband is wearing a three-piece suit, which lends him an air of great authority. Julia is slim and attractive, with a fashion model's pose, her left leg elegantly extended.

Other developments in the last quarter of the nineteenth century which must have encouraged the emigration of Najib and his brothers to Haifa were the improved roads linking Lebanon to Palestine and their enhanced security.

As I looked around A'yn Anoub I tried to imagine how Najib and his family must have lived. The presence of mulberry trees indicated that they raised silk worms and spun silk, as many villagers in Lebanon did at the time. They must also have produced and sold rose water and molasses, for which the Lebanese are justly famous. But how well could they have lived on such cottage industries? The up and coming cities along the eastern Mediterranean were Beirut, Jaffa and Haifa. At the end of the nineteenth century, when Najib moved there, Haifa had around 8,000 inhabitants, double the population of 1875. And the place was developing fast, especially once it became connected with the railway network that extended from Damascus all the way to the Hijaz. All in all, not a bad choice.

After descending from Fahd's rooftop, we had to cross a narrow plank spanning a deep ditch to reach the ground. He noticed me looking apprehensively at the flimsy plank. I admitted that I'm not too good with heights and would rather go down into the ditch and climb up the other side.

'Don't worry,' he said. 'It's only a short distance. I'll help you. Just follow me and give me your hand.'

I tried not to look down and reached out to him. He grabbed my hand and helped me across. We got on to a mound.

'Here on this spot was the original family house,' Fahd said.

'It must have been Najib's,' I muttered.

'Probably,' Fahd conceded. 'It's been a *khirbeh* [ruin] since I was a child,' he added. 'It was once larger. Then the road was built and took part of it.'

I wondered if it would ever be excavated. But who would want to do it besides me? Who is as interested in Najib's past as I am? Yet I am no archaeologist.

A fern tree was growing just below the mound.

'Has this always been there?' I asked Fahd.

'Yes, as long as I can remember.'

The tree did not look more than a few decades old. But it was clearly growing in what must have been the garden of the family of the *khoury* Jirjis, Najib's father. It had certainly been well nourished by the household's composted waste and the crumbled remains of the house that has now become a *khirbeh*.

Moving away from the mound, my eyes fell on a porch with columns and a balustrade. It belonged to a house that had had the same ironwork on the windows and doors, the same louvre shutters and style of pillars as the house that my grandmother Julia and her husband, Salim, had built for themselves in Ramallah. This porch was very nearly identical to the one where Julia used to spend most of her summer mornings.

'Whose house is that?' I asked.

'It belonged to Faris Nassar. He had no children and left the house to a charity to develop as a clinic for the village,' Fahd told me.

This was the house my sister Siham remembered visiting during our family trips to Lebanon that she had described to me. Oddly enough, I had no recollection of ever having been here. Perhaps because, with the legacy of loss in Jaffa and the numerous homes we had been forced to abandon, my mind was unwilling to accommodate yet another lost dwelling.

When we climbed up to the porch I saw a large limestone mortar in a corner, almost an exact replica of the one that is in my grandmother's kitchen in Ramallah. I remember the heavy wooden pestle that I had trouble lifting as a child. I also remember Julia sitting down on a low wicker stool, her knees clutching the mortar on both sides, pounding away at the meat to make the *kibbeh* (minced meat pounded with *burghul*, or cracked wheat, usually eaten raw) for which she was famous. The talent for making this delicious dish must have been passed down from her mother, Katbeh. In every house the Nassars inhabited they must have had that same large mortar.

I paced about the spacious balcony, taking in the view of the distant sea, so luminous and blue on this gorgeous winter's day. Perhaps Julia had this place in mind when she and Salim built their summer house in Ramallah.

'Where is the church?'

'Over there. Can you see it?' Fahd pointed to the north. He had no glasses and I with mine could hardly make it out, but I still said, 'Yes.'

Then I asked, 'Can we go see it?'

'Of course.'

Before leaving I stood facing the *khirbeh*. This mound of earth was all that was left of the original house of my Lebanese ancestors. I looked closely. I have seen many such *khirbehs* in the hills of Ramallah, but I'd never known the people who had inhabited them. Here was one that had belonged to a member of my own family. Perhaps, if it were excavated, kitchenware and implements might be discovered, or at least shards of pottery. But no one was ever going to dig here. It has no significance for the general public. It will remain one rather attractive small mound amid the neighbouring buildings, preserving within it the relics of a family that once lived here in the mid-nineteenth century, a family whose sons and daughters, their children and grandchildren, are now dispersed all over the world.

We had to drive to the church. Fahd had his car, but it was a shabby pick-up with all the tools of his trade in the back. He wanted me to go in the clean rental car that had brought us here. I politely refused, insisting on riding with him.

'It's a long way to come from America,' he said when we started up the hill.

'I don't live in America,' I said. 'I live in Ramallah.'

He was surprised. But now that he had asked I was not going to lie.

'But you mustn't say this to anyone,' he told me, regarding me with kind, concerned eyes. Then he whispered, 'Your wife is American. You must say you live in the States. Otherwise people will assume you come from Israel. It is not safe, especially with the Shia.'

'Are there many of them here?'

'The majority. We Christians are a minority in the village.'

After a pause I asked, 'Can we also visit the cemetery?' I had promised one of the Nassars who lives in America to say a prayer at his father's grave.

Fahd produced a large bunch of keys and looked for the one to the cemetery. I was impressed that he had it. We went in. To our left was an area where many Nassars were buried.

There were pine trees that rustled in the soft wind. I listened intently, trying to capture the spirit of the place. Then I walked away from the others and sat on a rock next to the Nassar graves. Eyes shut, I offered the promised prayer. This attempt at connecting with my maternal relatives through prayer made me feel closer to them than ever before.

Afterwards we drove a small distance further up until we reached the church. Again Fahd brought out his ring of keys, looking for the right one.

'So you have all the keys?' I asked.

'Yes, all of them. I have the keys to all the Nassar homes. The ones to the church, the cemetery. They all left the village and I remain, a keeper of the keys.'

I looked at the metal ring from which hung keys to padlocks, gates and doors of different ages, sizes, shapes and colours. They reminded me of the bunch of keys my mother had one day thrust at me, saying, 'Here are the keys to our house in Jaffa. Take them, they're yours.' I felt their weight as they landed on my lap. By then my father was dead and my mother must have been relieved to pass them on to me, and with them the hope of returning to the house where she had spent the first three years of her married life. I put them in a tin box and closed the lid, never expecting to open it again.

I strolled down the path lined with pine trees to the

nineteenth-century Greek Orthodox church, where Father Jirjis Nassar must once have officiated. It was an attractive church that had been recently renovated. It had a new reception hall in the garden outside, with beautiful views of the sea below. I circled the old structure and found stairs leading to the roof. I climbed up and surveyed the city and its most attractive bay.

When I went down I asked how many come to pray here on Sundays.

'Between ten and fifteen. The priest comes from Souk al Gharb.'

I didn't want to ask Fahd why he and his family continued in the Greek Orthodox faith. The pattern was a familiar one from Ramallah. Those Christians who had ambitions for education and life beyond their village, and who were willing to overlook the colonial aspects of Protestantism, switched allegiance, converting to the new churches that offered better opportunities for education and work in other lands.

Perhaps it was fortunate that one part of the family had stayed in the village, maintaining their attachment to the old church. Otherwise who would be the guardian of the keys?

As we passed Souk al Gharb, where Najib must have gone to school, I wondered what effect being a Protestant and member of a minority within a minority had had on Najib's politics. For one thing it meant that he got a decent education, which gave him a good command of English. This in turn gave him access to Zionist literature that was not available to non-speakers of a European language. The main source of his book on Zionism was the *Encyclopaedia Judaica* in English. It also enabled him to read what Zionist supporters were writing in newspapers in Britain and the United States. His educational background and church affiliation gave him the chance to work at the Mission Hospital in Tiberias, where his experience of being with the British left a strong impression on him.

And yet he was conflicted. Unlike the Muslim Sharif Hussein, he did not believe in the prudence of joining the British in the war against the Ottomans. He suspected that a British victory would lead to the colonisation of the country. Despite the accusation by the authorities of treason, he supported the Ottoman *millet* system. He was proud of being an Ottoman, which in his mind encompassed members of the three religious communities living in Palestine. He never considered turning his religious affiliation into a national identity. His identity was firmly defined as an Arab Ottoman.

It is not clear how aware he was of the irony of his affiliation with a church from whose British members emerged the first Christian Zionists. some of whom encouraged the secular Jewish Zionists to utilise the Old Testament in support of their struggle to colonise Palestine. Reliance by Protestants on the Old Testament and their insistence on its historical truth paved the way for the Zionist claims over Palestine. Was Najib aware of this heritage and could these conflicts and contradictions perhaps explain the guilty conscience that led him to work tirelessly in the cause of saving the land from the Zionist colonisers?

Without any hard facts about Najib's trip from A'yn Anoub to Haifa, I decided to travel south in an attempt to discover a route Najib might have taken, trying to recreate for myself a plausible version of the journey he made all those years ago.

Whenever Abu Rami, our driver, was tailed by another driver as he drove us south, he would slow down and wave the other car to go ahead: '*Itfadal, sidi* [please, sir], go, go.'

Along the way he pointed out where the Syrian check-points had been. 'Right here they had a camp. You see this clearing to the right? They pitched their tents there. The houses nearby, they took them over and stayed in them. They would stop us and make us wait. If they needed groceries delivered, they would order us to fetch them.'

Some of the crossroads which Abu Rami said had been held by Syrian soldiers were now manned by the Lebanese army. As he approached he always slowed down, lowered his window and politely and enthusiastically saluted the young men: '*Yateekum al afieh shabab* [May God give the young men strength].' And they would wave him through. I couldn't imagine how the Syrian army would have responded to the polite salutation of this softly spoken man. I also wondered when I would have the opportunity, if ever, of taking visitors around and pointing out where our army of occupation had been stationed and how they had behaved towards us. I was tempted to share this thought with Abu Rami, but I was not sure how much sympathy he felt towards Palestinians. Many Lebanese blame my people for their long years of suffering. Of course he was too polite and professional to show such feelings; we were on the best of terms. But then I was his customer and I was generously tipping him at the end of each day. He was a good driver and pleasant company. Why spoil it with talk of politics? From my point of view, it was best not to know what role Abu Rami had played in the civil war. So, prudently, we both avoided any discussion of the distant past.

'Look how the Israeli bombers have demolished this bridge. Just two precise hits and it was destroyed. Now we have to make a long detour.'

The destruction of a civilian bridge like this one seemed to me the essence of cruelty. But the speed with which the Lebanese had repaired so many of the bridges we crossed was evidence of the futility of such destruction. In our small area of the West Bank, Israel has for many years been destroying homes and institutions, and we have rebuilt them straight away. Sometimes we feel exhausted, but what society ever gives up on life because of attacks from a nearby enemy? The only experience the Lebanese have of Israel and Israelis is of bombings and destruction. How can Israel hope to gain acceptance from the people of the region where they have established their state? Have they no knowledge of history?

I asked Abu Rami whether we could leave the new highway and take the old coastal road.

I always prefer smaller roads. I hate the sound of rushing traffic. It makes me think of emergencies. On the smaller roads you can experience your surroundings, pass through villages and have the chance to observe people working the fields, trading in shops or sitting out sunning themselves. Why the rush, especially on this expedition, where I was trying to absorb the way things are in order to conjure up how things would have been when Najib made the same journey down the coast?

Abu Rami made a sudden stop and began backing up. I was glad we were not on the highway or we would have caused a major accident. On this narrow road it was safe to reverse like this. I didn't ask him why he was doing it, because I trusted him.

When we stopped at a small shop he exclaimed, 'I had almost forgotten.'

'Forgotten what?' I asked.

'Didn't you tell me you wanted to buy carob molasses? Here is the best place.'

It was a small shop with a roof of corrugated sheet metal. A few flowering shrubs had been planted on each side. The shop was run by a man and his wife. She was dressed in a dark *toub* like the one worn by Katbeh in Julia's old photograph. Big jars of molasses were displayed on a bench set outside the shop. The wife took the top off one of them and offered me a taste. She took a spoon and scooped some out. It was excellent, so much better than anything I could get in Palestine.

'I'll take a kilo,' I said.

Penny looked slightly distraught. 'How will we carry it back?' she whispered.

But I went ahead anyway. From experience I knew that the effort would be worth it. Once home we would be glad to have brought back the molasses. A kilogram would last us a long time.

How many of these jars would Ibrahim and Najib and their families have carried with them when they travelled south? Many, I should think. They would not have trusted finding the same quality of food in Palestine. The Lebanese have always cared a lot about their food and have special ways of preparing it, so that a dish prepared in Lebanon will be far more delicious than the same one prepared in nearby Palestine. This is partly due to the superior quality of Lebanese vegetables and herbs, which are cultivated in more fertile soil with an abundance of water. But it is not only the ingredients and manner of preparation that account for the difference. The Lebanese also display great talent in the presentation of food. There is a proverb in Arabic that says, 'It is the eye that eats.' Traditionally, all the restaurants in Ramallah that have acquired a good reputation can show a Lebanese connection, with either the wife or the mother-in-law of the owner coming from Lebanon.

After this short gastronomic stop we continued along the narrow winding road that followed the shoreline. We passed a large number of banana groves but as we got closer to the border with Israel I began to dread seeing the horrific damage wrought on the southern Lebanese villages during the Israeli invasion of the past summer. However, I was not allowed to reach them. We were stopped at a roadblock and told that only Lebanese citizens could pass through. This was meant to stem the flow of foreign volunteers and arms to the south, in a lame attempt at preventing Hezbollah from rearming after the latest Israeli invasion. The southernmost town we could reach was Tyre. Having failed to continue any further, we stopped there to visit the beautiful Phoenician, Greek and Roman ruins.

The largest and most impressive ruins in this city that, in 1984 was declared a world heritage site by UNESCO, is Al-Bass Archeological Site. Visiting it, I was expecting to delve into Lebanon's distant past but instead found myself confronted with a living tragedy. The Roman Necropolis which I saw first had a number of highly decorated marble and stone sarcophagi scattered over the ground. These and other relics were not marked and the paths were overgrown. There was a pervasive feeling of dereliction and neglect. Something was not right.

Walking eastward I passed the first of three triumphal arches that have managed to remain standing, two thousand years after they were constructed. I was heading towards the largest and best preserved Roman hippodrome in the world when a tree-sized red hibiscus on a raised ground to my left caught my eye. I climbed a few steps to get to it. As I stood in its shade I noticed two steel bars running over the ground. They were all that remained of the railway tracks that had once connected Lebanon to Palestine. One of the two extended further ahead, the other was plucked out, its severed end arching dramatically upwards. Looking in the direction that this track must have taken, I saw that it would have passed right through the Palestinian Refugee Camp, Al Buss, which bordered the Archaeological site. The train that once could have transported the refugees back to their homes had long since stopped running. This crowded camp, originally built in 1939 by the French government for Armenian refugees, now housed over ten thousand Palestinians.

As I examined this long since abandoned line, I could hear chanting coming from the Camp. It was 1 January and the residents were celebrating Fatah Day when the Palestinian revolution was launched. Earlier in the day we had tried to enter the camp, but were not allowed in by the Lebanese army checkpoint guarding the entrance. As I listened to the young people inside using loudspeakers to make their voices heard beyond the walls of their confinement, singing nationalist songs and delivering speeches commemorating the start of the Palestinian struggle for liberation, and occasionally firing shots into the air, I became uncharacteristically teary. I thought of my fellow Palestinians, refugees for over sixty years, confined to a small ghetto so far away from home, denied the right to work in most professions, prohibited from moving out of their camp, still hoping, struggling, dreaming of the day they would be able to return. I wondered whether any of them came from the village of Kawkab al Hawa in the Galilee, near the castle of Belvoir. How I yearned at that moment for the train that would one day travel again over this land connecting all the people living along the eastern Mediterranean as it once had done.

Not many years after Najib and his family loaded their belongings on to a cart pulled by two mules and headed south to Haifa, T. E. Lawrence, in typical British explorer fashion, hiked from Beirut to the Galilee along coastal paths that cannot have differed much from those used by Najib a few years earlier. This prolific and elegant writer described the trek in a letter to his mother dated 2 August 1909: 'I left Beirut not long after the beginning of July, and walked straight to Sidon (30 miles or so). It was very pleasant, along the sea-shore the whole way; beginning with sand-hills and mulberry plantations (for all N. Syria battens on silk-worms): it gradually improved to olive yards, and finally arrived at sterility and empty sarcophagi, at Heldua [the ancient name for the site of the present inn, Khan al Khalde].' The men he saw made him 'really feel a little ashamed of [his] youth out here' for at '16 [they are] full grown, with moustache and beard, married, with children and [have] perhaps spent two or three years in New York, getting together enough capital to start in business at home'. He describes the men as wearing 'baggy trousers, and short coats, or shirts, with a sash round their waist, but further from the coast they approximate the Bedouin dress: for head-gear, sometimes the fez, sometimes the *keffiyeh*, the black coiled rope of the desert Arab'. Many of them had visited America and could speak English, which, he says, 'they love to display before their fellow villagers'. He points out that many carried 'revolvers, some of them guns, and you see them ploughing in the fields, or eating at home in a belt of 150 cartridges: enough for a campaign'.

Like Lawrence, the Nassars must have stopped for the night in the houses of villagers along the way. These would mainly have been two-level mud houses with clay floors covered by mats made of long reeds, with the lower floor reserved for livestock, the upper for humans. The villagers were known for their hospitality to travellers and would have welcomed a family on the move, making room for them in their crowded space. There would have been no question of charging them for the accommodation.

Lawrence describes Sidon as having streets that are 'so narrow, and all built over above with houses: some were so narrow that 2 men could only with difficulty pass, and in others I had to bend even my head to pass: no wheeled vehicle can enter the gates. There are two castles, one standing on a mound of purple shells: neither very interesting: it is astonishing to see the number of antiquities dug out continually in Sidon: the neighbourhood is a perfect treasure ground.'

From Sidon Lawrence walked over what he describes as 'waterless hills' to Nabatiyeh, which he locates 'near the elbow that the lower course of the Litany [River] makes'. He lingers in the town, which was celebrating a festival, to observe the locals. 'The people in the shops chaffering over infinitesimal sums, sweet-meat sellers, the ice drink man who sells syrups, crying out "Take care of thy teeth" or "Refresh thy heart." Or the man with plain water in a goatskin with brass spout, then the fruit-sellers, "if an old woman eats my cress she is young tomorrow"; and funniest of all men with women's ornaments crying "appease your mother-in-law", and then as you are looking on at this comes a hoarse gasp of "dahrak" (your back) and a porter crashes into you with a fresh-killed sheep on his back, or a load of charcoal or perhaps a camel loafs through the crowd with its bell round its neck giving notice. If anyone neglects this warning they are knocked down like ninepins: camels seem irresistible. They are extraordinarily common at this season for all the corn of Bashan and the Hauran and Esdraelon is coming down to the coast, and all the nomads, who draw to the Jordan in summer for its water, hire out their stock to the farmers. It is very sweet listening to the ringing of the varied bells of a caravan of half a hundred camels in a valley: all the roughness of the tone, and the growling and grunting and cursing of the animals themselves, is lost at a little distance.'

I remember watching a camel drinking at a petrol station in the Jordan Valley. I was totally fascinated. As he plunged his head into the bucket provided by his devoted driver, his split upper lip demonstrated the most amusing convolutions, working energetically, opening and closing, trying to guzzle as quickly as possible the largest possible amount of water to store in the recesses of his vast body in preparation for the long period of abstinence. The beast was assisted in this endeavour by his floppy lower lip. When these lip exercises were completed the camel slowly lifted his head and from atop his long neck looked down imperiously at the rest of us, surveying the scene around him through narrow slanting eyes expressing patience and benevolence, his lips now pursed together in a broad, satisfied grin.

Typically, Lawrence's description of Palestine, which he first 'glimpsed from underneath a hill', admits no appreciation for the beauty of the landscape. Except for the high cliffs that mark the present border, there is not much difference and no natural boundary between Palestine and south Lebanon. People's physical features, their dress and dialect are as similar as the landscape. The two areas constitute a single continuous terrain. Lawrence writes: 'from on top one finds that it [Palestine] is all terraces and has been cultivated: now all the corn is cut so that all day one walks over varying greys, and browns, and whites, and reds, never a touch of green, except small thorny oaks or at times a fig tree where there is water under the surface: one does so rejoice in a spring!' He goes on to express his exasperation with the countryside: 'Palestine is all like that: a collection of small irritating hills crushed together pell-mell, and the roads either go up and down all the time, or wind in and about the rocks of the valleys, and never reach anywhere at all ... All day one steps from one sharp rock to another, which is not only tiring to the feet but to the brain also for one has to be continually on the alert, to find the best place for the next step, and to guard against slips. As a result one is soon satisfied with that sort of road. The alternative is a field path which is much better; these paths are very easily made and have an odd trick of dying away in the middle of a square mile of thistles from one to three feet high of a blue grey colour and very hard. To walk through them for any length of time is rather painful: one acts as a pincushion.'

In the spring of 2009 I took a group of Western writers participating in the Palestine Literary Festival on a walk in the Ramallah hills. Afterwards one of them, who was obviously not used to walking, described them as 'tiresome hills'. Fortunately he was in a minority of one. But then he had come unprepared, with soft shoes that are unsuitable for our stony hills. No wonder he couldn't enjoy the walk.

The annoying thing about the descriptions of many an English traveller in the Middle East is that they constantly look for their own English landscape or for a biblical landscape and therefore cannot see the reality around them. The only spots for which Lawrence has anything positive to say were the Jewish colonies, which he praised for their orderly appearance. And yet despite the huge differences in attitude and politics between Lawrence and Najib one realises how both shared a romantic vision that idealises the Bedouins. In later periods both looked back on the time spent in the wilderness as the best and happiest of their lives. Both also died disillusioned, feeling they had been betrayed by their own society, and disappointed at the defeat of the causes they had championed. They also witnessed and lamented the transformation of their Bedouin heroes, whom they had idolised as the most noble of human beings.

The Nassars might well have thought the coastal road still too insecure. They could have used the inland route instead, travelling first to Damascus and thence to Acre. Lawrence raises the issue of security of the coastal route when he reports the amazement of the villagers at finding him travelling on foot and alone. He writes: 'Riding is the only honourable way of going, and everyone is dreadfully afraid of thieves: they travel very little.'

To get some sense of this alternative route I asked Abu Rami to drive me to the Bekaa plain in the Lebanese part of the Great Rift Valley. We passed through a much more dramatic landscape than Palestine's. A gently sloping floor rises very gradually from the Bekaa towards the north and east. At its highest point, over 900 metres above sea level, stands the grand temple complex of Baalbek, one of the largest in the Roman Empire. The fault lines here continue to make adjustments, leaving this part of the Rift Valley subject to earthquakes. In 1758 a quake wrecked parts of the pagan temples. The vulnerability to major earthquakes extends further south to the Jordan Valley. To the east and west are mountain walls that rise between 1,500 and 2,150 metres and are covered in snow for a substantial part of the year, creating a spectacular panorama of a wide and fertile plain bordered by a mountain range on each side.

This Lebanon range is the highest of the mountain massifs east of the Mediterranean. The highest peak, Qornet es Sauda, east-south-east of Tripoli, is just over 3,000 metres, while Mount Sannin, east-north-east of Beirut, is only 300 metres lower. As in Palestine, the rocks here are mainly porous limestone. The water from the rainfall they absorb is forced to the surface, producing many springs at unusual altitudes of between 900 and 1,500 metres above sea level. Unlike the springs further south, many of these are forceful, creating rivers capable of irrigating large areas. This, together with the fact that the soil here is very fertile, is why the middle slopes of the Lebanon range are intensely cultivated.

We drove through a landscape criss-crossed by deep ravines and forbidding cliffs often hundreds of metres high. The difficulty in penetrating inland from the coastal plain must have rendered these areas the perfect refuge for persecuted religious minorities. This was why different groups survived here with a measure of autonomy during Ottoman times, as no others were able to do in the Middle East. The fragmentation of Lebanese society along denominational lines has continued even after the state was established and has led over the years to terrible civil wars. When I asked Abu Rami for the names of the villages we passed, whether it was Zgharta, famous for its *kibbeh*, or Zahleh, with its exquisite riverside restaurants, I was often reminded of some gruesome massacre that had taken place there at one point or another in Lebanon's bloody history.

As we drove south through the Bekaa I tried to keep in mind that this plain was a continuation of the Dead Sea, through Lake Tiberias, and the Huleh plain. To the east was the Lebanon range, to our west the Anti-Lebanon and, at the southernmost tip, the 2,830-metre-high Jabal al Sheikh (Mount Hermon).

When we got to Lake Qaraoun in the Rift Valley I was overcome by an overwhelming sense of melancholy. The troubles and possible massacres that drove away my great-great-uncle have never been resolved. They were in abeyance, dormant for a while as the forces on the different sides renewed their energies during the respite. I asked Abu Rami to park and wait for me as I walked down the hill to the lake. There was only one single motorboat on it and a few abandoned houses along the path. There wasn't a soul in sight. I wanted to touch the water of one of the few lakes in the region that wasn't in Israeli hands. When I got to the shore I stooped down and tried to listen, letting my fingers relax in the cold water. Except for the faint hum of the distant boat there were no other sounds. The water hardly moved. After a short pause, I stood up and looked eastward. The snow on the summit of Jabal al Sheikh in the Israeli-occupied Golan Heights hung like clouds in the blue sky.

As I stood by the lake I had to struggle to convince myself that what I saw on my left was indeed Jabal al Sheikh; that a drive of one hour would take me across the Golan Heights, Syrian territory under Israeli occupation since 1967; and that from there it is but a short distance to the Galilee, the arena of Najib's escape, and then home to Ramallah in another two hours. During Najib's time none of these borders existed. He travelled with an entirely different sense of a landscape than the one which has since become fixed in my mind and my contemporaries' by years of distorted history, colonisation and nationalism. I found I had to make an effort to distinguish between what is physically possible and what is practically impossible. The political fragmentation has made these lands unbridgeable. As I stood looking at the sight familiar to me from the Israeli side of the border, I realised that a new map of the Middle East had truly been created and that, much as I try to free myself, I remain trapped.

8

The Arrest

Najib slept at the mouth of a cave overlooking Wadi al Bira. When he opened his eyes he saw a straight-backed horseman looking down at him. He remembered seeing this horseman before. The rider dismounted and they shook hands.

'Why are you sleeping like this in the open? Have you been granted amnesty?' the man asked.

'I'm no criminal to be forgiven. I have decided to give myself up,' Najib answered.

'Then listen to me, my friend. I know people whose houses are at the edge of the wilderness. I can take you to them. Get up and let us ride together and deny Jamal Pasha the satisfaction of your arrest.'

'I thank you for your concern, but if I don't give myself up they will arrest my friends and torture them. Is it right that others who were kind to me should suffer on my behalf?'

'Let those who build houses lament their destruction. You come with me to the safety of the wilderness.'

Najib stood still, thinking, unable to make up his mind.

Despairing, the Bedouin said, 'I have nothing further to say except to wish you good day.' And with this he leapt back into the saddle and rode away, his horse racing with the wind.

Najib gazed after the horseman as he disappeared into the distance, envying him his freedom. Was he a fool to leave these open fields and deliver himself into the soldiers' hands? Was he ready for their rough treatment, the confinement of prison and perhaps ultimately the hangman's noose? 'I must be mad to give myself up and lose all this,' he thought. He stood up and began to mount. In his novelistic account he writes that he then remembered his friends, although he makes no mention of his family, his estranged wife or his children. He imagined his friends being led by soldiers to the detention centre to await the train that would take them to the military court, where they would surely be tortured and accused of treason for helping a traitor. No, he would never be able to live with himself. He felt his foot slip out of the stirrup and he sat down again, supporting his head in his hands. Then, despite himself, he fell asleep.

He was awakened by his nephew when the sun was about to set. He stood up, put his foot in the stirrup again and mounted his steed, riding ahead of the other three without anyone saying a single word. They all felt that his hour of reckoning was approaching.

They continued to ride in silence for three hours, until it was completely dark.

Now Najib asked, 'How much longer till we reach Nazareth?'

'Perhaps an hour,' his nephew replied.

They decided to go first to the house of his brother Rashid. He was not greeted with great jubilation, but with a palpable sense of relief, as though a burden had been lifted off his hosts' shoulders.

In the morning he was brought a new suit and shoes. He had only worn sandals for almost three years. He shaved his beard and was now ready to appear before the governor.

The moment the governor saw him he erupted. 'Where have you been? We've been searching for you for three years.'

To which Najib answered simply, 'I was in hiding.'

'And why hide at a time when loyal citizens should be working with the government to save the country?'

'I hid out of fear of injustice.'

'Are we unjust?'

'I have been calling for an Arab union under the general umbrella of Ottomanism. I have also been resisting the Zionist movement with every ounce of my being. Working as I did to realise these aims, I made many enemies. I was worried they might spread false rumours about me and in these critical times the military officials might reach a hasty decision against me and I would end up dead.'

Impressed by the fact that Najib was giving himself up voluntarily, the governor decided not to detain him pending his transport to Damascus, where his trial would take place.

Najib remained in Nazareth receiving well-wishers for three days until, on the fourth day, he received a telegram from the *mutassarif* of Acre summoning him for interrogation, following which he would be escorted to Damascus to appear before the military tribunal.

Had Najib been arrested just a short time earlier he would have received much harsher treatment. But by the time he gave himself up in 1917 the Ottoman rulers had become aware that their policy of hanging Arab leaders was alienating the Arabs and driving them to side with the Allies in the war. It was widening the rift between Arabs and Turks and depleting the country of Arab leaders who could play a more positive role in supporting Ottoman rule. The active participation of Sharif Hussein in the war on the side of the Allies both disappointed and worried the Ottomans. Najib's memoir was written during the British Mandate period, after the collapse of the Ottoman Empire, when the popular perception of that period was generally negative, and yet in describing the investigation he was subjected to in Nazareth he emphasises the respect reserved for Arab dignitaries and the kindness with which he was treated. He might have been thinking of how this contrasted with the way British officials treated Palestinian rebels opposed to the Mandate. Reading his account made me think of how much worse is the treatment afforded by Israel to those accused of resisting the occupation or that of the United States in Iraq. In all my experience of Israeli military courts I have not one memory of an Israeli judge being prepared to listen to reason, or being swayed in the slightest degree by the persuasive eloquence of the accused or their defenders. They follow their instructions religiously and punish whoever appears before them regardless of age and with blind efficiency, never remembering that the two nations will ultimately have to find a way of living together. Najib endured his ordeal, and still experienced humanity and mercy, during a devastating world war under a regime generally regarded as autocratic and devoid of respect for those standards and principles of human rights that are proudly advocated by super and regional powers claiming to be democratic.

Whenever Najib mentioned anything that the investigating officer believed would be used against him, he was advised to change his tune. At the end of three days his papers were ready and arrangements were made to transfer him to Damascus, where he would appear before the military tribunal. Before he left, his friends were able to raise fifteen pounds for him and provided him with change of clothing and a horse.

After bidding his brother and friends farewell, Najib rode down the hill east of Nazareth. At the outskirts of the town he met the policeman from the Zoubi family who had stopped him on his way to Kufr Cana and nearly arrested him. This time Najib introduced himself truthfully and reminded the officer of the incident. The policeman claimed that he would not have arrested Najib if he had identified himself properly. To prove his goodwill he went on to say, 'If you would like to escape now I will accompany you wherever you wish.' To which Najib answered, 'If I had wanted to escape I would not have given myself up after living in the safety of the wilderness.'

He continued riding with the Zoubi to Afula, across the spacious Marj Ibn Amer plain with its surrounding hills. Galloping through, he succumbed to morbid self-pity, comparing himself to Christ travelling for the last time to Jerusalem to be crucified. 'But at least his people met him with jubilation and decorated his path with palms,' Najib told himself. 'Who will cheer me and reward me for my services to my people?' He continued in this vein: 'How often have I fought to keep these lands in Arab Ottoman hands? Is there anyone now who would save me from the oppressor Jamal Pasha if he should decide to crucify me?' But then he remembered the number of good men like Abdullah Fahhoum who had gone out of their way to help him, and was able to lift himself from his despair.

Reading Najib's novel, I remembered similar words being uttered by my father, who often complained of having done so much for his people without appreciation. After his tragic death my mother could not reconcile herself to her loss. She continued to ask why he had sacrificed his life for such an unappreciative society. In my later years I hope I will be spared such pointless grumbling.

At Afula Najib was kept under guard until the train arrived. That night he travelled by steam train, accompanied by an Ottoman officer, arriving at Dera'a in the morning. There they remained for an hour before resuming the journey to Damascus, arriving one hour after sunset. He found the city festooned with banners and streamers to celebrate some German victory against the Italians in the war.

Najib asked the officer whether he wanted to hand him over that same night or whether he could spend the night at a hotel.

'As you wish,' the officer replied.

Thinking of the hardship and discomfort awaiting him, Najib decided to pamper himself by spending the night at the Damascus Palace Hotel. But when he asked for a room the manager looked him up and down, noting the armed officer behind him. He did not like the look of Najib, nor the fact that an officer was with him.

Najib could see this and smiled, saying, 'I was born to suffer.'

'I am very sorry but we are full,' the manager said.

Najib said to the officer accompanying him, 'Let us go where they will welcome us. Off to prison.'

But the prison would not have him because the official who processed new arrivals was not available. So Najib was taken to a military camp, where he spent the night in a tent, with the soldiers sleeping on the floor. Next day he was taken to Muhamad Ali Faydi, a man with a squat figure, dark complexion and small black eyes whom Najib knew from Haifa and with whom he'd had long conversations about patriotism. He had since been promoted to Head of Battalion.

Now when Najib was presented before him he pretended not to know him.

'Who are you?' he asked Najib in his Egyptian-accented Arabic.

When Najib answered he asked, 'And when did you arrive here?'

'Yesterday,' said Najib.

But the officer did not like the way Najib answered. In a loud, commanding voice he ordered him to turn his face and leave the room. Then he called for more soldiers to be summoned. When eight of them had arrived he hurled his orders at them in Turkish, placing his hand on his sword as if he were preparing for battle. They stood as ordered, in formation, two in each row with Najib in the middle, flanked by four soldiers in front of him and four in the back. Again he was presented to the commander, who, in a voice as authoritative as if he were ordering a whole battalion to go to war, told them to march. Under this heavy guard Najib was taken to his cell at Khan al Pasha, the prison of the military court.

Through the small door they entered a vaulted vestibule that led to the courtyard, which was lined with rooms that had been used as stables for the horses, with the upper rooms rented by the travellers for accommodation. Those prisoners who were in favour were kept upstairs; the rest were put in the stables, to which Najib was now taken. He was strip-searched and his money and other possessions were taken away. The stout Anatolian guard with a dry way of speaking, whom Najib says turned out to be kinder than he first appeared, recited to him the rules of his incarceration: 'The prisoner may leave his room twice a day only. If he should speak or even gesture to any of the other prisoners or try to bribe any of the guards he will be shot at once.' The warden then stooped down and whispered, 'I warn you not to violate any of these rules, for I have received orders to treat you in the most severe manner. I have never received stricter instructions than these.'

The door was closed and Najib began inspecting his cell. Wood shavings were placed on the floor to cover the animal droppings. On the wall he found two nails and by the window looking out to the courtyard a large stone. He studied these and thought they might come in handy if he was treated so harshly that he decided to hang himself. That night he could not sleep. The harsh treatment he got gave him reason to worry about his future. The floor on which he slept was damp and fetid. Damascene nights at the end of autumn were cold and all he had for warmth was his thin cloak. Towards midnight he heard the voice of Muhamad Ali Faydi, who had come to warn the guards to be especially vigilant with Najib. As soon as he left, the guard came to check the lock of Najib's cell and ascertain that he had not escaped.

Najib spent fifteen days in this cell, leaving it only to use the toilet and speaking to no one. Then one day the warden appeared at the door and asked whether he needed anything. Najib said yes, he wanted to write a letter. Once the warden had brought pen and paper, Najib wrote to Jamal Pasha Junior, reminding him of how he had promised to help when Najib appeared before him in Nazareth.

'I am now at the Khan al Pasha prison,' he wrote, 'and in dire need of your help. Is it right that I should be treated as a criminal even before the court has condemned me? I can understand receiving such harsh treatment after my conviction, but not when I have not yet been found guilty.'

Two days passed and Najib was summoned to appear before the military tribunal. The indictment against him was read. There were fifteen counts, including the accusation that he was opposed to the Unionists and consequently to the Turks, the state and its German allies. Also included was the charge that he had authored the letter deposited in the post office mailbox at the German Colony in Haifa threatening that the people would surrender to the British unless the Ottoman government made concessions. Moreover, he was accused of spying for the British, the enemy of the Ottomans in the war. More than any other, it was this charge that alarmed him. If found guilty of this alone, he would surely be condemned to death by hanging.

After Najib pleaded not guilty to all the counts, his trial began. He was asked by the president of the court, 'Did you call for the support of the British?'

Najib gave his usual answer, expressing his honest position that 'the Ottomans should never have entered the war and I called for neutrality. But after the war began I wrote that a man remains free to voice his own opinions until his country participates in a war. Then he must speak in its voice, look with its eyes and listen only with its ears.'

He was next cross-examined at length about the tremendous amount of intelligence that had been gathered concerning him. He was even asked his reasons for changing his son's name from Anwar, after the Ottoman commander, to Adeeb. He patiently argued in his own defence, always speaking as truthfully as he could. This examination dragged on for twelve sessions. At one point the court requested that the files regarding the accusation about the letter he was charged with writing be ordered from Jerusalem so that a comparison could be made between the handwriting in that letter and Najib's. Once this was done, Najib was acquitted of this charge. But his trial continued, as did the harsh prison conditions he suffered.

It was only after the intervention of Jamal Pasha Junior on his behalf that the restrictions placed on Najib in prison were eased. He was moved to a different prison with other prisoners, whom he soon learned had already been tried, found guilty and condemned to die. For Najib to be among condemned men was a trying experience.

In one of the cells in which Najib stayed he met a Jewish convict awaiting death by hanging. During his last two nights the condemned man had developed a fear of the dark, but with the guards' help he had managed to buy candles, which he kept lighting one after the other until daybreak. Najib felt sorry for him and decided to stay up to keep him company. In the course of their conversation the man revealed to Najib that he had boldly declared before the tribunal that what he did was done not as a spy or out of treason, but in the service of the Jewish national cause.

Najib was deeply moved. He also learned for the first time that Jews had joined the war on the side of the Allies with a special Jewish unit known as the Jewish Legion, which was trained to be part of the British Army. This was not unlike what Sharif Hussein of Mecca was doing, fighting on the side of the Allies. But could the Sharif not have heard of the Balfour Declaration, in which the British had promised Palestine to the Jews? Could he have consented to have Palestine ceded from the rest of the Arab world when it gained independence after the defeat of the Ottoman Empire? Najib did not know what to believe.

He continued to be brought before the military tribunal, which examined the evidence against him. Once on the way to the court he was pushed by the guard and treated so harshly that he felt he could not take it any more. He stood before the judge and asked, 'How long will my ordeal last?' The judge told him to shut up, saying, 'You stand before us accused of the most serious charges and you have the temerity to lecture us? We will not tolerate any more speeches from you.' At which point Najib answered, 'If your court denies the accused of the right to defend himself and to appoint a lawyer, then here I stand before you. Pass whatever verdict you see fit and let us finish with this trial.' At this point the judge changed his tone and replied, 'Of course you are free to defend yourself as you wish. Speak.' But Najib couldn't. He said he was too emotional, having been treated badly on his way to court, and he asked for an adjournment.

Once back in his cell, Najib began to plan what he was going to say at the next session. He was deep in thought when he became aware of the warden standing by the door, asking him to put on his clothes and follow him. He feared the worst. But he soon found himself standing before a civilian policeman, who then took him to see Khalil Rifaat, who had served as president of the court in Ajloun, a town on the eastern bank of the River Jordan.

At first Najib did not recognise him, but the judge said he knew about Najib and his patriotic position, reminding him that they had met in Haifa. 'Once I heard that you were being held in the prison in Damascus,' he said, 'I immediately went to meet Jamal Pasha Junior and told him of my high opinion of you. The Pasha asked me to convey to you that because of the seriousness of the charges against you only the General Commander can make a decision in your case. Many have poisoned his mind against you. But the commander is soon to be transferred to Istanbul. Once Jamal Pasha Junior takes his place he will make sure to acquit you. Until then he has asked that your trial continue to be adjourned. All you need to do meanwhile is to remain patient and not to despair.'

Najib was comforted to hear this. Prison conditions were severe but now that the end was in sight he was better able to endure them. One day, as he was having his supper of a small piece of bread and a few raisins, the warden appeared and told him the news that Jamal Pasha Junior had taken over, winking knowingly at Najib, for he knew what this would mean to him. A week later the news of Najib's acquittal finally came. It was conditional, though, upon his assisting in editing the newspaper *Al Sharq*, the mouthpiece of the Ottoman government and its allies in the Great War. It was printed in Damascus, the centre of press propaganda, rather than Istanbul, because the city was the meeting place of pilgrims before their journey to the Hijaz. The newspaper was part of a systematic campaign to counteract the Hijaz uprising led by Hussein Ibn Ali. Najib was given back the clothes and the few coins that had been taken from him when he was imprisoned. Everything was returned to him except the piece of bread he had had with him when he was taken in. To him this was evidence of the level of hunger the Ottoman soldiers were enduring.

In his novelistic account he writes that he never fulfilled this condition. The reasons he gives for his refusal reveal a puzzling attraction to and admiration of the British, of whose policies towards Palestine he was already aware. He writes that his refusal was not 'because I was unwilling to serve the Ottoman state, but because of my good feelings towards the English. I believed that they would not do any work unless it was for the good of humanity.' He then adds that through mingling with them 'for a number of years in Tiberias I came to know of their good principles and behaviour and read many literary books by their great writers and novelists. Shakespeare's nation could never undertake any action that might harm the refined cultural values for which it was famous. I also believed that the Ottoman government committed a grave error in participating in a war against them.' It is true that this was written while he was already living under British rule, yet it was not like Najib to curry favour with rulers. He was more in the habit of writing and speaking his

mind honestly and truthfully and suffering the consequences.
He does offer another reason for his refusal, writing: 'I did not
find it right that I end up serving the German policies that I
initially refused to serve and for which I sacrificed the future
of my children, the life of my family and many other material
rewards and for which I risked my life.'

Although Najib was out of prison, he could not leave
Damascus without a permit. It took repeated interventions
by numerous friends and well-wishers before he was able to
secure a permit to take the train back to Haifa. At this point
he had his children with him. In his account Najib makes
no mention of who brought them to Damascus, how they
managed there or his feelings about being reunited with
them. Neither does he mention his wife and whether he
made any effort to find and bring her back. The only reference
to the children comes in his description of the trip back to
Haifa, when he writes that before reaching Afula they heard
the buzzing of a plane. The train stopped and the passengers
climbed down, dispersing over the plain and lying on the
ground. He writes that he 'made each one of [his] children
lie far from the other so that if bombs are dropped and one of
them is hit the others would be spared'. But when the pilot
realised the passengers were civilians, not soldiers, he flew
away. Soldiers then were more merciful to civilians than they
are now. Najib and his children made it to Haifa, where he
prepared for the relaunch of his weekly newspaper *Al Karmil*.

On 9 December 1917, shortly after Najib returned to
Haifa, General Allenby, commander-in-chief of the British
Expeditionary Force from Egypt, occupied Jerusalem. This
was followed in 1918 by the conquest of the north of Palestine.
The Ottoman forces defeated, the battle for Palestine was won
by the Allies.

The country the British occupied had been devastated

by war. The people of Palestine paid dearly for the European decision to use their land as a theatre of war. Almost 40,000 Muslims, more than 10,000 Christians and more than 1,000 Jews had fallen victim to tyranny, gunfire, famine and disease. The 800,000 inhabitants who were left were immediately classified by the new rulers according to religious affiliation: 650,000 Muslims, 80,000 Christians and 60,000 Jews, including both the veteran Jewish *millet* and the recent Zionist settlers, with the remaining 10,000 being of different religious sects. The immediate consequence of the war was the disappearance of Turkish officialdom and language. It was as though the Ottomans had never existed. For middle-class people like Najib, educated at the English missionary schools, there would be new rulers using a language they could speak well and espousing liberal values which they believed meant that the new rulers would help their country to catch up with the rest of the world.

In 1920, the year when *Al Karmil* resumed publication, the British replaced military rule with a civil administration. They appointed a high commissioner instead of a military governor to take charge of the country. Meanwhile, the Zionist movement was working hard to make the vague promise of the 1917 Balfour Declaration the basis of the British Mandate over Palestine. Deliberations on the final map of the new Middle East began in San Remo in Italy in 1920. From that time until the conclusion of deliberations in 1922, Zionist diplomacy was fervently active. Lord Balfour was recruited to head an Anglo-Zionist committee to lobby for the implementation of his 1917 declaration. The Americans were persuaded not to oppose the inclusion of the Balfour Declaration in the charter for the Mandate for Palestine. In September 1922 a clause was added to the charter excluding Transjordan from Palestine and defining the Mandate as extending from the

River Jordan to the Mediterranean Sea. This meant that with the three sub-provinces fused into one administrative entity Palestine became more united administratively than in the Ottoman period. While waiting for final international approval of Palestine's status, in 1923 the British government negotiated the final borders, thereby generating a clearer sense of belonging to the people living in it.

The 1922 Mandate for Palestine was created as a 'Class A Mandate'. This was defined by Article 22 of the League of Nations Covenant as 'territories that had previously formed part of the Ottoman Empire and that had reached a stage of development where their existence as independent nations can be provisionally recognised subject to the rendering of administrative advice and assistance by a Mandatory until such time as they are able to stand alone.' The British Colonial Secretary clarified his view of this provision as the self-determination of Palestine, explaining that 'Palestine should be developed, not as a British colony permanently under British rule, but as a self-governing state or states with the right of autonomous evolution.'

Yet only the minority Jewish population, constituting less than 10 per cent of the population of the country, was promised self-determination. Article 2 of the Mandate left no doubt about this. It stated that 'the Mandatory shall be responsible for placing the country under such political, administrative and economic conditions as will secure the establishment of the Jewish national home ...'

The Mandate began on 24 July 1922. Its inauguration did not seem to have plunged Najib into despair, as one might have expected. He still believed it would be possible to win the struggle against the establishment of a Jewish homeland in Palestine. The 60,000 Jews living in Palestine then owned only a tiny proportion of the land. It was never the policy of the Mandate to expropriate land and hand it over to the Zionists. Jewish settlements had to be established on legally purchased land. This must have given Najib hope that the struggle to prevent the establishment of the Jewish homeland in Palestine could be won. It was why he poured his energy into the fight against the sale of land to Zionist Jews.

Although colonisation meant control and exploitation, the infrastructure put in place to achieve this was useful. Rural Palestine became less isolated. Trains and trucks brought telegraph and mail services to almost all the country. During the late Ottoman period international mail had been taken to Jaffa to be shipped to Europe, but now post office branches were opened everywhere. A public telephone network was installed early on, old roads were repaired and asphalted, and the railways were extended to a number of new stations.

Two months into the Mandate, Najib took the first of many trips throughout mandatory Palestine and Transjordan to report on the state of the region which had now been fragmented into two political entities. Each of his dispatches he called a 'letter'. Twenty-three of them appeared in 1922 and a further sixty-three in 1925. Not only were these reports from the field a pioneering style of journalism in Palestine, but they also provide an unrivalled source of information about the economic, social, cultural and educational conditions that prevailed during this most crucial transitional period. From these letters we learn that travel between the villages in the north of Palestine, which used to be unrestricted, now required a passport. Whereas the whole area was once known as Syria, it was now divided into Syria and Palestine and a passport was required for travel between the two. Najib praised the authorities for granting free passports to facilitate travel between the villages, which, he said, had many ties between them. But he complained about the customs barriers that had been erected, because these hampered trade and the movement of goods, especially sheep. In his letter from Safad he described how, as a result of these political divisions, this northern city had lost much of its commercial significance as a trade centre to Kuneitra on the Golan Heights in Syria and to Bint Jbeil, now part of the Lebanese territory placed under a French Mandate.

In one of the letters published in 1922 Najib wrote: 'Wars are of different kinds and the war that is being waged these days in Palestine between the nationalists on the one side and the Zionist Jews on the other is an economic war that also takes different forms. What we are facing today is competition over the ownership of the land. We left Jenin at the tip of the Marj Beni Amer plain from the south and travelled north in the direction of Nazareth and were faced directly with the front because *Khawajas* [the gentlemen] Sursuq, Twaini and Khoury sold and are selling their property in Al Yajur, Kufrata, Jadruo, Tabooun, Sheikh Buriek, Tel al Shumam, Jeeda, Fula, Afula, Jabata, Khanefis, Tel al Adas and others and have delivered them to the enemy thereby relinquishing by their own accord their right for notability and national leadership. Nothing of their status as nationalist in any Arab country is preserved for all these countries shall be harmed in unequal measure as a result of the establishment of the Jewish kingdom.'

Some of the letters described villages such as Saffuriyya which were entirely razed by Israel after 1948. In letters from Beisan, Tiberias and Nazareth he reported on how demoralised he found the inhabitants of the villages in these regions as a result of the sale to Jewish buyers, on behalf of Zionist agencies, of land that included a number of entire villages. In a letter published in 1925 he wrote: 'Hearing is not like seeing. Whoever passes by those lands on both sides of the road between Haifa and Nazareth and sees how some of them have been transferred to the Jews and others are on the way to being so transferred, and sees the local national workers replaced by Jewish workers, cries out like women at a country wasted by the quasi men through their negligence and indulgence in places of pleasures and absence of manliness and weakness of national principles and can no longer retain any respect for such people.'

In another letter he described the Jordan Valley as 'a pot of gold' which if properly developed could produce wonders. But he found its people lazy and the government not doing enough to develop agriculture there. On one of his visits to Beisan he felt nostalgic for the time he had spent with the Bedouins who had been so hospitable to him during his flight, and he decided to pay a visit to the Bashatoeh tribe.

In the letter he wrote from there entitled 'A night in the goat-hair house', he expresses admiration for the sheikh of the tribe and how well he was able to summarise the prevailing situation. The sheikh told Najib that the Jews could not extract from the Arabs what the Arabs did not wish to give, nor could they seize Arab land against the will of its rightful owners. 'It is we who sell our land to them,' he said. He then asked, 'Was it not Sharif Hussein who brought the English to our land by striking an alliance with them? It was he who led us to fight the Turks and gave us large amounts of dynamite to attack the railway line repeatedly. Therefore we are the ones who brought these strangers into our homes. If we do not sell them our land they will not come to own our country.'

Najib was impressed by the sheikh's wisdom and his analysis of the prevailing situation. He was in full agreement and believed that if the Arabs refused to sell their land to the Zionists, the Mandate government would fail to achieve its aim of creating a Jewish homeland in Palestine. This was why he dedicated himself to advocating support for farmers and lobbying against the sale of land to the Zionists. But censorship had not stopped with the British. On several occasions the Mandate government prevented Najib from publishing his newspaper. Obdurate as he was, he proceeded to publish blank pages with only the nameplate appearing on top. His supporters bought the empty pages out of solidarity.

When he could publish, again and again he resolutely took up issues related to land sales. Reading them made me realise that I had found a kindred spirit. I could see the similarity in our belief that it was within our power to oppose, through civil action, the policies of the government controlling Palestine and prevent it from fulfilling its objectives. After 1967 I shared Najib's optimism about defeating the policies of the occupying power of taking over Palestinian land for the establishment of Jewish settlements. I believed that through the legal struggle it would be possible to frustrate the Israeli policy of colonising the land.

Both Najib and I were non-combatants who saw our role in the realm of advocacy: I through the law, my great-great-uncle through journalism. In retrospect I realise that we both attributed too much significance to our form of struggle. Time proved that it was not the sale of land by Palestinians to Zionists that ultimately enabled them to create a Jewish state in Palestine. It was the combination of war and driving the Palestinians out by force of arms that made it possible. Likewise in the Occupied Territories with the settlement project. It soon became evident that Israel was bent on seizing Palestinian land and was using a veneer of legality to conceal its actions. My legal struggle had little impact on the settlement policy. Even after it was affirmed in a report sponsored by the Israeli government that 40 per cent of the settlements were established on land that Israel acknowledges as privately owned by Palestinians, nothing was done to remove them. To my great dismay, law and legality did not prove to be decisive weapons in our battle against Israeli colonialism.

The occupation that began in 1967, when I was sixteen years old, and gave Israel control over the rest of Palestine was treated by successive Israeli governments as a continuation of the Mandate that ended in 1948. Only this time it was the state of Israel, rather than Great Britain, that was the self-appointed mandatory power. Israel never made public its intentions, even when each and every Israeli government pursued the same aim of using its full control over the Occupied Territories to settle Israeli Jews and expand the borders of the Israeli state by eventually annexing them. Both powers proceeded early on to make changes in the local law to realise their objectives. The British started the land registration process, giving priority to coastal areas and the Galilee, where the Zionists were intending to settle, to help purchases with a clear title. The Israeli military government in 1967 suspended the process of land registration that had begun with the British and relied on the ambiguity of the borders of unregistered privately owned land to claim it as public. This was made available to members of the Israeli public in violation of the international law of occupation, which prohibits the occupier from settling its own population.

Faced with challenges similar to those Najib had encountered earlier in the century, I believed that we needed to work as hard as we could to entrench our presence on the land, just as Najib had argued in many of the 'letters' he published in his newspaper that only by improving the conditions of the *fellaheen* could they be helped to hold on to their land. For me and my generation *sumoud* (steadfastness) was the operative word. Only through *sumoud* would we be able to prevent Israel from taking our land and annexing it. And like Najib, after years of working for the cause and borne along by the great hope offered by the First Intifada, which began in 1987, I too suffered a profound sense of despair when it came to an end.

Now, forty-odd years after the occupation began, when I look at our hills in the West Bank, so full of Jewish settlements, I see the contrast between the ancient Palestinian villages spread out on the slopes and in the wadis and the new settlements placed on top, planned with an eye to military considerations in the way they relate to each other, to the main roads, to the sources of underground water and the manner in which they are encircled by wire fences. It has taken me all this time to see how militarised our hills have become and to grasp the obvious: one side lives as though the land will always be theirs, whether or not they are able to defend it, and the other is building strategically placed fortresses in preparation for the time when the opportune conditions arise for pushing the Palestinians off their land, as was done in 1948. Perhaps, like Najib, I was too involved in the civilian aspects of the struggle to notice its most fundamental nature. Now it has become clear to me that whatever the legal excuses utilised to enable these settlements to be established, they were but a façade, mere packaging that encouraged Israeli Jews to believe they were not taking anyone's private land. The tragedy is that this war strategy, which guided Israel's actions and was fundamental to its struggle to colonise the country, never developed into a strategy of peace even after Israel achieved statehood.

One result I had not expected from delving into the life of my great-great-uncle was a better understanding of and sympathy for the cause of the Bedouins. It was the statement that his friend made in Wadi al Bira when he was trying to persuade him not to give himself up – 'Let those who build houses lament their destruction' – that struck a deep chord. What he was telling Najib was to let those who live a settled life take responsibility for it, while the Bedouins had made other choices. Perhaps we in Palestine/Israel who have built houses and are suffering the consequence of our blind possessiveness over the land and the narrow national agenda to which we adhere should learn from the alternative Bedouin outlook.

We haven't yet. Nor are we ever likely to, for one of the tragic consequences of the scramble to possess land following the Israeli occupation was that the Bedouins were pushed out of their traditional grazing grounds. Most of us failed to see that they represent an alternative, attractive way of life and attitude to land that we must all have once shared and from which we still have much to learn.

In 1925 Najib, the loyal Ottoman citizen who had been hoping and working for greater Arab independence within the empire in which he was born, was made a Palestinian citizen. This was by virtue of Article 1 of the Mandate, which stated that 'Turkish subjects habitually resident in the territory of Palestine upon the 1st day of August, 1925 shall become Palestinian citizens.' But His Britannic Majesty could not decide whence he derived the power and jurisdiction over Palestine that empowered him to bestow Palestinian citizenship on the former subjects of the now dismembered empire far away from Britain, so the enactment gives a laundry list including treaty, capitulation, grant, usage, sufferance 'and other lawful means'. The British were acting as colonialists. They couched their actions with a veneer of legality, just as the Israeli military government did after 1967, but acted on the strength of their position as conquerors. With the support of their allies they proceeded to treat the dominions of the former Ottoman Empire as their own to give away as they pleased.

In 1927 Najib married Sadhij, the granddaughter of the Grand Baha'i, the founder of the Baha'i religion. Najib had been her Arabic teacher. She was thirty years younger than him and one of the most militant leaders of the women's movement in Palestine, described by the British authorities as a 'very dangerous woman', a 'menace to public security' and 'a prominent agitator' who had 'organised a number of demonstrations attended by violence'. While his wife continued her militant activism, Najib seems to have become more despondent. A Jewish writer who met him in 1933 wrote: 'Najib opened his heart to me and told me of the disappointment he feels from the lack of appreciation by his own people for what he has done for them and his struggle extending over many years against Jewish settlement. "Had I been one of you," he told me, "you would have given me my due of appreciation more than my Arab brethren."' A similar sentiment was expressed by my father, who also felt under-appreciated by the people he dedicated many years of his life to serving and believed the Israelis were better at giving credit to those who served them. Few Israelis would agree with this.

There was another conquest in 1948. This time it was the Zionist forces that captured about 75 per cent of the territory of Palestine under the British Mandate. As a result of their victory they were able to force out most of the Palestinian inhabitants of the Galilee. One hundred and sixty-six villages were demolished in the four sub-districts. All of the Bedouin encampments where Najib had stayed were cleared away and the vast majority of Bedouins were compelled to move to the eastern side of the river. Najib died in March 1948. He had been suffering from severe diabetes and was depressed and demoralised, spending much of the year in the town of Beisan, close to Tiberias, on his banana farm. He was buried in Nazareth. In the early 1980s my father used to say that the way things were going there would not be enough land for a Palestinian to find somewhere to get buried. Perhaps it was fortunate that Najib's death was just months before the Nakba, before Palestinian citizenship was cancelled along with Palestine, and before the long, seemingly interminable struggle to restore it was born. If death could ever be considered a blessing, a good case can be made of Najib's. Perhaps it was better to die than suffer the fate of the rest of his family, who lost everything they possessed in Haifa and became destitute refugees in Lebanon. At least he was able to make sure that his remains stayed in Palestine.

Najib's brother Ibrahim, who owned the Nassar Hotel on Street of the Kings in Haifa, had died a few years earlier. His sons, Anis and Farid, were running the hotel together. His sister, Lydia, had moved to Nazareth after she got married and was running the Royal Hotel there. In 1948 they were all forced out of Haifa and Nazareth. The Nassars were scattered in the surrounding countries. Julia, Najib's niece and my grandmother, ended up in Ramallah, while her brothers and mother went to Beirut. Najib's second wife, Sadhij, left with their only son, Tawfiq, for Beirut, where she eventually died. Tawfiq ended up as a journalist living in Damascus. Najib's first wife was never heard of again.

The fall of Palestine proved detrimental not only to its Arab inhabitants but also to the land itself. The new Jewish state that emerged proceeded to rapidly eradicate as much evidence as possible of the Arab presence on the land and to accommodate millions of new Jewish immigrants from different parts of the world, including survivors of the Nazi Holocaust. Very quickly the entire country was reinvented. Huge projects were undertaken that caused irreversible damage to the environment. Tributaries of the River Jordan and the river itself were diverted, reducing the flow of water into the Dead Sea to a trickle, causing the salt sea to begin to dry up and changing for ever another segment of the Great Rift Valley.

One of the tenets of the Zionist ideology behind the creation of the Jewish state was that the land of Palestine under the control of the Israeli army would be placed inalienably in the exclusive ownership of the Jewish people. To this end, 93 per cent of all the land on which the Israeli state was established in 1948 and 60 per cent of the West Bank occupied in 1967 were registered inalienably in the name of the Israel Lands Authority and the Jewish National Fund, both of which are prevented by law from selling it to non-Jews. Such exclusivist practices and ideology can only be sustained at a great price. Rather than integrate in the region and make peace with its neighbours, Israel has to remain in a high state of military preparedness, ready to defend the gains it has made through war and keep at bay the Palestinians it refuses to allow to return to their homes or to compensate for their losses. In time its people will grow exhausted by the burden of having to defend an ideology that eventually will become untenable and impossible to justify and sustain. Something will have to change, but whether or not it will come from within Israel itself is an open question.

On the way back home from Lebanon, a small incident took

place as we were crossing the Allenby Bridge back to the West Bank.

I had just passed through the metal detector, having removed, as ordered, everything from my pockets, including my house keys, wallet and the leather belt I was wearing. Retrieving my belongings, I made the mistake of putting on my belt before picking up my wallet and keys. I had just buckled the belt when I felt the hands of the Israeli woman soldier pushing me away. I tried to reach for my wallet but was ordered not to touch anything. Something had happened that made these soldiers behave as though they had been bitten by a rabid dog. I tried to insist that I would move only after taking my wallet, which contained my passport and other documents, and my keys. But there was no way I could reason with them.

Along with all the other travellers we were swept like dirt to the other side of the lobby without being given any explanation. For forty-five minutes I waited anxiously, certain that when allowed to return I would find neither my wallet nor my keys.

Meanwhile I tried to discover what could be taking place but was given no explanation and was told to keep away. Finally we were allowed to return. Fortunately, I found my possessions where I had left them, untouched. I discovered that some warning light had flashed when a hunchbacked old man who hardly seemed to have the energy to walk had passed through. This had frightened the soldiers and led to the fuss. Looking at those soldiers, one would have thought there was a major incident. It turned out to be nothing that could justify such a strong reaction.

Usually when travelling through Israeli borders I keep my calm no matter what. But this time I was unable to control myself.

'I'm going to tell them off,' I announced to Penny, and began walking towards the female soldiers guarding the entrance.

'What are you going to say? Where are you going? It's all over now. You'll just stir things up and cause more delays. Come back.'

'No. I must.'

'You're mad, I tell you. Come back.'

I refused to listen to Penny and went right up to the two women soldiers.

'You're sick,' I bellowed at them. 'Can't you see it, and can't you accept that you are overreacting? If I am right in my diagnosis then you need psychological counselling. Why don't you ask the Americans to send you money for a new NGO to help you? They pay for everything else.'

Penny was pulling me back, pleading with me to be quiet, to calm down. But having started, I could not stop. I went at them with the passion of the Old Testament prophet Ezekiel, someone who had seen the light and had to put his point across.

Unlike my Nassar relations, I am not blessed with a strong, booming voice that carries. With all the surrounding commotion of the noisy terminal full of travellers only a few of the soldiers could hear me. And all they did was to look at me blankly without flinching, for they were well trained. Then eventually one of them uttered the magic word, 'TERRORISM', pronouncing it in that distinctive Israeli accent popularised by Ariel Sharon, using the velar 'r', so that what came out was 'teghoghism'.

'What about terrorism?' I demanded to know.

'Haven't you heard of teghoghism?' she asked.

'I have,' I said, 'but what I've seen has nothing to do with that. Many other countries have to deal with terrorism and they don't behave in such a deranged way.'

But I was not heard. Eventually one of them lifted the phone to report to her superior in a laconic, unperturbed manner, 'One of them is making a *balagan*.' I knew the word in Hebrew. It means 'mischief'.

Her description of what I was doing made me realise that I could have said whatever I wanted – neither Penny nor I had to worry – and I would not have been heard. For that to happen she would have had to abandon the foundations on which she constructs her world and her ability to act within it as a superior human being with a superior cause towards an inferior human being, a congenital terrorist, unruly and incapable of civilisation, who cannot accept his place in the scheme of things set up for him in which she plays her part very well and very properly, without having to think or to feel any pangs of conscience.

Nothing I could say would be taken seriously. Israel's racism towards me as an Arab was of the modern sort. It was not based on what I did or said but on who I was, a Palestinian Arab, and therefore in their eyes an inferior being, 'one of *them*'. Unlike Westerners who criticise Israel, I didn't have to worry about being accused of anti-Semitism. I should have known that it was a waste of my energy to attempt to communicate with those who do not attribute an equal status to me as a fellow human being, a lesson that all victims of discrimination under colonial regimes over the ages have had to learn.

Once I breathed deeply, as Penny had been suggesting, and looked around me, I wondered how many of us 'underlings' have developed contrary racist attitudes, as some Israeli Jews did against anti-Semites in old Europe, blacks against whites in America or South Africa, and Arabs against Jews in the contemporary Middle East, and knew this was my big challenge and what I must guard against. Otherwise I ought to find my way back to Lebanon or the West and live another life before I'm ruined.

As we crossed the bridge and drove into my occupied land the numerous checkpoints and the abominable wall came into view. I recalled the words of the eminent Israeli historian Benny Morris: 'Palestinian society is in a state of being a serial killer. It is a very sick society. Something like a cage has to be built for them. There is no choice. There is a wild animal there that has to be locked in one way or another.'

I used to think that it was Kafka's novel *The Trial* that most aptly described our situation under occupation, with the myriad military rules that confine us. Now it appears that to some Israelis we've become like Gregor in the short story *Metamorphosis*, waking up one day to find that we've become disgusting creatures whose closest neighbours have to keep us confined in a cage.

9

Welcome to Nazareth

During the three years I spent writing this book I thought that the only way to capture Najib's past was by using my imagination. There was no possibility of visiting any of the houses where he lived, seeing any photographs of his family or examining any sort of memorabilia. Other than his writings, all evidence of his past life in Palestine had been turned into rubble. I walked through the Galilee hills in silent communication with the ghosts of the past, trying to read beyond what was now visible, excavating the tremendous changes that have been carried out in the course of a determined effort by Israel to eliminate any evidence that the exiled Palestinian Arabs ever lived there. But then, as I was writing the last chapter, an email flashed on my screen from a relation I had not known existed. Lydia lived in the Galilee. She explained that her grandmother, after whom she was named, was Najib's sister and that she, along with her father, were the only descendants who continued to live in

Haifa after 1948. In one of my books she had read about my grandmother Julia, one of Najib's nieces, and expressed an interest in meeting me.

Lydia was four years old when the Nakba took place. Her father was working for the Iraq Petroleum Company and the British owners transported him and his family to Beirut by plane. Lydia's grandmother, who owned the Royal Hotel in Nazareth, went with them. After spending a few months in Lebanon, her father and his immediate family were transported back to Haifa by the company. But Lydia's grandmother was not allowed to return. Despite passionate letters written by the son to David Ben-Gurion, the Prime Minister of the new Israeli state, on behalf of his mother, she was never allowed back and her hotel and other properties were expropriated. She died in Lebanon, never having set foot in the country or seeing her son and his family again.

A few months later I arranged to meet Lydia in Nazareth, where she now lived with her husband, Yusuf Tabar. The trip north was fraught with the usual uncertainty of present borders and sadness of the past. When we arrived at our hotel, Lydia called. Her first words were simple: 'Welcome to the Galilee.'

This struck me as a wake-up call. So far my trips to the area had been an escape into a land where no one knew me. Once Penny and I had deposited our bags at the hotel in Tabgha, at the northern tip of the Sea of Galilee, we would change into our hiking gear and take the car to the start of one of the many walks in the hills of the Lower and Upper Galilee. Driving along small roads to begin our walk, the pastoral below-sea-level landscape of the lake would give way to a spacious green valley and forested hills. How we relished the uninterrupted drive without the checkpoints and barriers that blight our enjoyment of similar excursions through

West Bank roads, moving in a dream world where, except for chance encounters, no one knew us.

One of our favourite walks was in the valley known as Wadi al Lymoon. It had once been the site of carefully tended orchards for the city of Safad, until 1948 a mixed Arab Jewish city, now exclusively Jewish. The valley was still full of the lemon, pomegranate, fig and olive trees planted by Palestinian farmers before 1948. Here streams continued to flow throughout the summer, so that fish could be found swimming in the puddles that formed along the way. It was by far a more bountiful land than the dry, much less fertile West Bank.

In these verdant hills of the Upper Galilee, we sometimes came upon the ruins of a Palestinian village where one or two Arab houses were somehow allowed to stand. We would stop before them, thinking of the lives their former inhabitants must have enjoyed in this green valley. Many have ended up in cramped refugee camps in Lebanon, living in miserable squalor, the 'generation of the Nakba', as they call themselves, passing away without seeing these places ever again.

It is a source of both hope and concern to me that I am capable of selective memory to enable me to endure the tragic present, wearing blinkers that blur what is painful and block it from my mind and vision. Yet even with my long experience of such survival tactics, my silent communication with the land would all too often be brought to a rude and decisive end. No mask could obscure a group of Israeli schoolchildren shouting and clapping as their teacher made them stop before an Arab ruin to explain the Israeli version of how it came to be there, as the armed guard accompanying them stood by, his eyes searching the hills for possible attackers.

But on this visit Penny and I were not planning to take another of our walks in the hills. This trip was going to be different. I had come to the Galilee to visit a relative who had found a way of living in crowded Nazareth, the only Arab city in Israel, where she has forged a life out of what she and her family were allowed to keep and, in the best Nassar tradition, was now the proud manager of one of the finest hotels in the city.

When I had mentioned that I was going to visit, Lydia treated me as she would any other tourist who comes for the first time to her area. She wanted to take me to the holy places in Nazareth, to see Haifa and drive up to the spectacular most northern point in the country, Ras al Nakourah, the gorgeous cape overlooking the Mediterranean Sea. I wrote back that all I wanted was to see and talk to her and her husband and visit Najib's grave.

I was struck when I first saw Lydia by her resemblance to my grandmother Julia. Both had a strong, open face with a wide mouth and a gap between the two front teeth. Lydia's eyes were blue and shiny and her light hair, which fell to her neck, framed her face. She wore a cross beneath which dangled a gold necklace. She was well and tastefully dressed. Her nails were painted red. I remembered how my grandmother continued to paint her face and nails well into her eighties. The resemblance also extended to character. Both women were articulate, wilful and sociable.

My first impression of Yusuf was of a mournful person who had been harassed by his strong-willed wife into accompanying her to this meeting with these strange and demanding relatives who had suddenly emerged out of the blue. He seemed withdrawn, had tired eyes and restricted himself to an occasional grin. Clearly he could have done without this interlude in the middle of his work day. My impression that he must have been through difficult times was strengthened by the missing front tooth, revealing a conspicuous gap when he opened his mouth. He was of average height, with a slight stoop. After we had spent some time together, the grin was replaced by a smile that covered his face and made his eyes sparkle. I realised that he was a perceptive and sensitive man, contrary to my initial impression. He might have been through hard times but he had not been defeated. Beneath that shock of white hair and bushy pepper and salt eyebrows was a warm, intelligent person. When he smiled his face opened up and took on a kindly look.

We had started our walk into what is still called the Kawar Quarter, where Najib went into hiding during the First World War. As we strolled through the narrow alleys, I asked Lydia about her childhood after her family returned from Lebanon. She told me that her father lost his job and for a long time remained embittered at not being able to find work. She grew up in Haifa, where she had only Jewish neighbours, went to a Jewish school and mingled with few Arabs. She was so pained by what she heard of the experiences of her Jewish neighbours, who showed her the numbers which the Nazis had tattooed on their arms, that she felt they had a right to a state of their own. In the marketplace of Haifa, because of her fair complexion, blue eyes and the light colour of her hair, Lydia would be mistaken for a Jew and she came to think of herself as an Israeli, not a Palestinian.

But when she moved to Nazareth and was surrounded by Arabs this changed. She became much more aware of the discrimination against the Arab citizens of the state that defined itself as the state of the Jews. 'Now when I ask my grandchildren,' she told me, 'they invariably describe themselves as Palestinians, not Israelis.'

I wondered whether Lydia's husband, Yusuf, grew up feeling the same way. His answer surprised me. 'We cannot speak of identity,' he said. 'We are not a normal people. We started off as the Arabs of Israel. To the surrounding Arab states, we who endured the greatest difficulties to remain on our land were considered to be enemies, a fifth column who was shunned and looked upon with suspicion. To the Jewish state we became the Arab minority. Then we graduated into becoming the Arabs of '48 and later the Arabs of the inside. Who are we? Palestinians? Arabs, Israelis, Christians, Muslims? What is our relationship to the Palestinians living under the Palestinian Authority, to those in East Jerusalem or to the refugees in Arab countries? Lydia has properties from her father's family in Lebanon. But is she allowed as a fellow Arab to take back her property, let alone visit? Of course not. As holders of an Israeli passport we can only visit a few of the Arab countries. And yet we are citizens of a state that defines itself as a Jewish state and excludes us from full citizenship, even when we constitute a quarter of the population. We face discrimination in all sorts of ways. Are we Israelis? Are we Palestinians? Are we Arabs? We simply don't know. We are not a normal people.'

As Yusuf spoke I thought that his description could apply to all Palestinians. We have become so torn apart that it is difficult to describe us as a normal people. Arab regimes in the surrounding states might not openly view us, the Palestinian residents of the West Bank, as a fifth column and prevent us from visiting, yet they remain suspicious of us. Outwardly they attribute great heroism to us for enduring Israeli brutality, never tiring of expressing great admiration at our resilience. Yet when our towns and villages are subjected to brutal attacks by the Israeli army, the solidarity of the Arab governments never goes beyond words of sympathy. Those that have signed peace agreements with Israel did not even bother to withdraw their ambassadors from Tel Aviv when Israel was waging its brutal attack on the Gaza Strip in 2009.

After this digression, Yusuf was beginning to tell me about the descendants of the Kawar family, who are still living in Nazareth, when a young man approached us.

'I heard you speak of Kawar. Are you related to them?' the man asked.

Ahmad Mardat was the director of an important Nazareth archive and a student of the Ottoman period. He knew a lot about Najib and the old families of Nazareth and used every opportunity to learn more. When he saw us he thought we might be relatives of Kawar from abroad, coming to visit Nazareth, and could perhaps help him with his research. As we continued on our walk through the alleys of the old city, exchanging what we knew about Najib, he told us about his work in trying to preserve the archives relating to the history of Nazareth and the Arab presence in Palestine. Whenever he heard of libraries belonging to some of the older residents of the city he would visit and search through them for whatever old books, documents or photographs he could find. But he lamented that a lot had been destroyed.

'When the residents of Nazareth learned that the Allied armies were approaching their city,' he told me, 'they believed that the soldiers would carry out searches of their homes. Anyone in possession of any document with the insignia of the Ottoman Sultan would be assumed to be a supporter of the old regime and punished. So they began taking out all the documents they had and burning them.'

It must have been the same fear that led Najib's brother to dig out the manuscript Najib had placed in a tin can that he buried in the garden.

As it turned out, we were fortunate indeed for this chance meeting with Ahmad, since neither Lydia nor Yusuf had the faintest idea where Najib was buried. From Ahmad we learned that the grave was in the Orthodox cemetery.

'But how could this be?' I asked. 'Najib was a Protestant. He should be buried with the Protestants.'

Though Ahmad knew much about Najib, he had not been aware that he was raised as a Protestant. I remembered reading that Najib had taken part in the conferences convened by the Orthodox congregation in the course of their long and bitter struggle to win independence from the hegemony of the Greek patriarchs, a struggle that flared up in 1921 with Najib's active support. I mentioned this to Ahmad.

'This doesn't prove anything,' he said. 'The Orthodox invited to these meetings whoever was capable of assisting them in their struggle, including Muslims.'

Why, then, was he buried with the Orthodox?

It was Yusuf who provided the most plausible explanation. He reminded us that the Protestants in the Middle East do not allow divorce. 'The Protestants would not allow Najib as a divorcee to marry Sadhij. But the Orthodox would. So he joined the Orthodox Church.'

Now that we had figured this out we were able to walk with confidence to the Orthodox cemetery.

Visiting the grave of a dead relative is not something that I would normally do. I have never been to visit my father's grave in Ramallah. It was different in the case of Najib. Here in this cemetery was the only evidence that I could see of his presence in the Galilee. Nothing else was left.

We had a hard time finding his grave. We had to manoeuvre through the narrow spaces between the tombs in this cemetery, which was as crowded as the living city. Then, under a ficus tree, in the shadow of the raised burial plot of the Kawar family, we found what we were looking for. It was a simple tomb made of two rows of limestone blocks with a rough headstone. The inscription there indicated that the tomb had been renovated in 1989 by the Council of the Orthodox Congregation as 'a tribute to the deceased Najib Nassar on the occasion of the forty-first year of his death'. On the tomb itself the following words were carved: 'Here lies the Sheikh of Palestinian journalism *Ustaz* [teacher] Najib Nassar the owner of *Al Karmil* newspaper who died on 30 March 1948.' It was a simple bleak tomb with no ornamental carvings or dressed stone. Many of the graves around Najib's were built-up and several of them had carved marble head-stones. Najib's did not stand out and was no different from those of the simplest folk. This would have pleased him. He would not have wanted it any other way.

I stood respectfully by the tomb, trying to be silent, but nearby two men were digging a new grave. 'For our *khityara* [our old grandmother],' they told me when I approached them to ask if they knew where Najib was buried. They neither knew where his grave was nor had ever heard of the man.

Most of those buried here lay with other members of their family. But not Najib. As in much of his life, he has remained alone in death. Most other members of his family had died outside Palestine and did not have the right to be buried in the land where they were born and would probably have wished to be laid to rest. His wife and son were buried in Lebanon and Syria. It was only because of the fortunate timing of his death that Najib could be buried in the land he worked so hard to save. As I stood by the grave, my thoughts went to another important Palestinian literary figure, Emile Habibi, who managed to remain in Palestine after the Nakba and on whose grave is the epitaph he chose: 'I stayed in Haifa.'

The past cannot be revived. The suffering that Najib and his descendants have endured cannot be undone. My hope is more modest: that travellers to and inhabitants of the Great Rift Valley, along the eastern Mediterranean Sea, whether in the Occupied West Bank, where it is imprisoned between Israeli checkpoints, in Israel or further north, where it is fragmented by numerous political borders, will lift up their eyes and try, as I did, to imagine the whole of this valley as one, a land without borders where everyone is free to travel and enjoy all the wonderful pleasures it has to offer. Those able to succeed in looking with new eyes might share my experience when writing this book, of a momentary rift in time, a respite from the terrible confines of the dismal present. After all, change only comes thanks to those, like Najib, who are capable of imagining a different world.

Acknowledgements

The production of a book goes through many stages. After a long and lonely process of conceiving and writing the manuscript, the contribution of many friends and colleagues followed. As always my first reader was my wife, Penny, who gave me good critical and editorial advice, in addition to emotional support and encouragement. The manuscript was then reviewed by my dear friend, Alex Baramki, who exercised his extensive editorial skills and rummaged through thousands of archival photographs at the Library of Congress. My agent, Karolina Sutton gave me good advice and professional assistance. The excellent eye of my publisher, friend and editor Andrew Franklin helped shape the book. Lesley Levene, my excellent copy editor, caught numerous errors and made excellent suggestions that have enriched the book. My historian friend, Bishara Doumani, kindly read the manuscript. And finally the proofreader, Carol Anderson, read through it with her outstanding professional eye. The managing editor at Profile, Penny Daniel, went through numerous archives searching for more photographs and oversaw the editorial process to bring out the book in its present shape. My thanks to Ruth Killick, publicity director at Profile, for all her excellent work in publicising the book and to all the staff at Profile Books.

In the course of researching the book and traveling to the various regions that this book covers I was helped by a large number of people all of whom I thank. They include: Salim Tamari who provided me with a photocopy of Najib Nassar's hard-to-find memoir, *Mufleh al Ghassani;* Sauheil and Mounir Nassar for their help in sharing their memories of Najib and the Nassar family and providing me with the Nassar family tree; Fahd Nassar for inviting me to his home in A'yn Anoub and showing me around the church and the village; Walid Shehadeh for his company during trips to the North of Jordan in search of Najib's route and offering a hand while I was slipping down into a ravine on one of our walks; Hani Bilbesi who drove me to the Galilee and was patient as I went examining sites along the way; Abu Ahmad my driver in Jordan and Abu Rami my driver in Lebanon for sharing their stories with me; Huda Zureik for providing access to the library of the American University of Beirut and to the staff of the library for their assistance; the staff at the National Library of Scotland for their assistance to me while researching the book and reviewing the maps; my uncle Fuad, cousins Nadeem and Kareem and partners at my law office for assuming extra burdens during my many absences, making it possible for me to take time off to research and write this book; Ramsey Abughazaleh for his hospitability and the photo of the school; John Viste for being such a wonderful companion on my last trip to A'yn Anoub and for taking pictures of the village; Susan Rockwell for her good cheer and stamina on a blisteringly hot walk in the Galilee and for photographing those vanishing rail tracks in Tyre; Ahmed Marwat for his help in Nazareth and for providing me with archival pictures; Lydia Tabar and her husband Yusuf for their generosity and for sharing family stories and showing me around in Nazareth. And finally for my mother, who died before this book was completed, for her prodigious talent at storytelling which brought me so much pleasure and guidance.

List of Illustrations

Frontispiece: A Bedouin man and his horse at the Makhada (Library of Congress)

1 Najib Nasser
2 Sazaj Nasser
3 Family portrait (author's own)
4 A Bedouin encampment (Library of Congress)
5 Haifa *c.* 1927 (Library of Congress)
6 Tiberias *c.* 1911 (Library of Congress)
7 Modern Tiberias, 2000 (photograph © Hanan Isachar/ CORBIS)
8 Aerial view of the River Jordan (Library of Congress)
9 Crossing the River Jordan near Jericho, 1866 (photograph by H. Phillips, reproduced with the kind permission of the Palestinian Exploration Fund)
10 Allenby Bridge, 1967 (Bettmann/CORBIS)
11 Endor/Ayn Dor (American Colony, Library of Congress)
12 Bekaa Valley, February 2006 (photograph © Ivan Vdovin/JAI/CORBIS)

List of Illustrations

While every effort has been made to contact copyright-holders of illustrations, the author and publishers would be grateful for information about any illustrations where they have been unable to trace them, and would be glad to make amendments in further editions.